The
Jeweled Menagerie

The
Jeweled

SUZANNE TENNENBAUM AND JANET ZAPATA

Menagerie

The World of Animals in Gems

Thames & Hudson

We lovingly dedicate this book
to our husbands, Michael and
Ricardo, and to our four-legged
companions who give us their
uncompromising love.

Conception and captions © 2001 by Suzanne Tennenbaum
Texts © 2001 by Janet Zapata

First published in hardcover in the United States
of America in 2001 by Thames & Hudson Inc.,
500 Fifth Avenue, New York, New York 10110

Library of Congress Catalog Card Number 2001086841
ISBN 0-500-51049-0

Printed and bound in Singapore by C.S. Graphics

Contents

Introduction

From the Ancient Egyptians to the Renaissance

Animals have been part of mankind's artistic repertoire ever since prehistoric man drew simple, yet amazingly realistic images of horses, bison and mammoths on cave walls. Since then, animals worn on the person are seen in all cultures and in every stratum of society. In ancient times, images were rendered naturalistically with specific meanings ascribed to different animals for amuletic purposes. Many centuries later, elements of animal facial features were rendered in more abstract designs. By the time of the Renaissance, elaborate enameled and gem-set confections featured animals still playing allegorical roles. It was not until the nineteenth century that animals were used solely for their decorative effect in jewelry design. Against this general background, it seems that to fully appreciate the beauty and value of jewelry with animal motifs, it is essential to delve into its history since the inspiration for many modern design images comes from the past.

In early cultures, animals worn on the person or interred with the deceased conveyed specific meanings that were obvious to everyone at the time. Some were ascribed evil deterrent, or apotropaic qualities, while others symbolized specific animal behavior or represented the character of omnipotent gods and goddesses. In a world that often seemed puzzling or overwhelming, recognizable images of animals helped the ancients to make sense out of confusion and to deal with events and circumstances that appeared to be out of their control. Each culture favored animals indigenous to its area whose behavioral characteristics people associated with superstition or magical powers.

The daily rotation of the sun is understandable to most of us today, but was mystifying to the ancients. The Egyptians, observing the industrious scarab as it rolled a ball of animal dung many times larger than its body to its underground hiding place, associated it with Re, the sun god who, they thought, rolled the solar ball across the sky as a daily routine. The scarab was also associated with regeneration since it was believed that it came into being inside the ball of dung (which, in reality, protects its eggs and larva). Thus, the humble dung-beetle became so revered in ancient Egypt that its image was carved into seals, an essential part of daily life, as they were used to secure property from theft and to validate legal documents.

Besides the scarab, ancient Egyptians used representations of a plethora of other creatures for a variety of practical and religious purposes. For example, turtle, scorpion, crocodile and vulture icons protected the wearer from the creature represented. Creatures whose image suggested desirable animalistic qualities included the bull for its savage strength, the cow for its procreative abilities, the frog and the lizard for their regeneration, the hare for its fertility, the hedgehog for its rebirth, the lion for its fierceness and bravery, the grasshopper for its association with wealth, and the monkey for its symbol of love and sexual fulfillment. Special connotations were bestowed upon the falcon and the cobra, both associated with royalty: the falcon, king of the sky, as the sacred animal of the king of the gods; and the sacred cobra, or *uraeus*, worn on the headdress of Egyptian rulers, as the symbol of their sovereignty.

Whereas in Egypt animal figures were worn mostly as amulets or to denote royalty, in ancient Greece, jewelry with animal imagery was also viewed as adornment in its own right. For Greek women, such jewelry was a means to enhance their appearance so as to attract the opposite sex. For Greek men, jewelry symbolized power and potency. Lions and lionesses, rams, bulls, snakes, stags, antelopes, fish and dolphins, frogs, cicadas, scarabs and, from the mythological world, griffins, horned lions and Pegasus graced gold jewelry from the classical period. The snake, besides its traditional role as a symbol of both the underworld and eternity, also served as a purely decorative ornament, taking advantage of the suitability of the serpentine form to wind itself around arms and fingers.

Another ancient culture, the Scythians from South Russia, portrayed animals in an entirely different manner: posing passively with heads and legs dangling, rear legs folded over the front legs, or curled into a circle. The most common images seen in their jewelry are the reindeer, stag, horse, real and mythological birds, griffins and felines, including the panther, lion and snow leopard. Images comprised the entire animal or a selected part, such as the head, that symbolized the essence of the animal.

The Celts never comprised a country or nation in the conventional sense but their unique stylistic traditions spread throughout Europe during the Roman period. Their jewelry is unlike earlier forms because, with a cooler climate than that on the eastern Mediterranean, Mesopotamia and Egypt, it developed as a functional complement to their clothes. The most common forms were pins and brooches that served as cloak-fasteners worn on one or both shoulders. During the early period in the sixth and fifth century BC, these were decorated with a single animal such as a dog or ram but, by the second half of the second century AD, a different kind of brooch came into existence based on the penannular form. The ornamentation lavished on these items is remarkable for its inventiveness and complexity. Animal images were no longer treated figuratively; rather, abstract zoomorphic features of an animal's eyes, ears, snout and head decorated the surface.

By the medieval age, European jewelry with animal imagery had evolved to more sophisticated designs using cast images, some enameled and set with precious gemstones. Design motifs included religious allegories, such as the pelican in her piety and St George and the dragon. Dragons, viewed as symbols of the demonic along with griffins, were seen on girdles and belts of the period.

In the late sixteenth century, towards the end of the Renaissance period, designs had become bold and quite ornate in the form of fanciful compositions, frequently enameled and set with precious gemstones and pearls. The stimulus of new materials imported from the Far East and the Americas as well as a great interest in and fascination for pagan mythology and ancient history, culminated in a new, imaginative art form adopted widely throughout Europe consisting of pendants that featured real and mythological animals. Although these pendants were meant to be worn, many were designed in a three-dimensional manner that made them more suitable for display in a *Kunstkammer* than for personal wear. A typical pendant was designed in a triangular form whereby two chains supported the central animal figure, the overall design accented with pearls either hung independently or strung as part of the supporting chains.

In Spain, animals represented within the Renaissance pendant tableau included exotic birds, lizards, dogs, lions, and creatures of the sea such as hippocampi and dolphins, their bodies enameled and set with Colombian emeralds or made with large, uniquely shaped baroque pearls. Designers of some of these creatures of fantasy were inspired by artifacts from lands conquered in the New World and depicted them in a ferocious manner with webbed feet, curled tails, sharp teeth and forked tongues. Others chose these images because of their allegorical nature, for instance, the dog for its fidelity, the lion for its strength and the unicorn for its purity.

The Renaissance was indeed a prolific period for the arts. Jewelry designers looked everywhere for ideas and inspiration. Mythology narratives, such as Europa and the bull, and Venus and her mermaids with dolphins, were well represented. French designers drew inspiration from paintings of the period: two mounted warriors in combat recalled the imagery of Leonardo da Vinci's sketch, *The Battle of Anghiari*; Phaeton driving the sun chariot was based on Francesco Primaticcio's *Phoebus and Diana*. In Germany, animal imagery included griffins, lions and warriors astride horses, while St George slaying the dragon remained a popular and pervasive image.

Although the allegorical significance inherited from earlier cultures has persisted as an element in the design of animal jewelry, sheer beauty and "fun" have increasingly become the features that attract most customers to the jewelry houses. This is a fascinating development that the rest of this book explores in some detail, amply illustrated with outstanding examples from each period.

Chapter 1

The Nineteenth Century
Revivalist, Victorian, Edwardian

At no other time in the history of jewelry was there such an explosion of innovative styles and techniques as in the nineteenth century. It was a time when everything novel was in vogue. The "new", or what was regarded as the new, arose in response to the demand from an emerging middle class that craved the latest fashions and, with the fruits of the Industrial Revolution, had the means to acquire them. That demand was satisfied by talented jewelers at the forefront of design, introducing new trends into the jewelry repertoire. Nowhere is this more evident than in the selection of subject matter. Flowers, ever popular in jewelry design, continued as a major design source but the period also saw an emergence of the animal as inspiration, either resurrected from past eras from Antiquity to the Renaissance or created from original designs, some ascribed with sentimental or symbolic meanings. As a result, in the latter half of the nineteenth century there appeared a plethora of animals, fish, birds, insects and fantasy creatures that crawled, slithered or ran across shoulders and veils or wound around arms, necks and fingers. Almost every species from the animal kingdom was replicated in some manner into jewelry design.

Many factors contributed to this interest in animals, from notable events – including the unearthing of ancient tombs or the opening of the Suez Canal – to man's interest in sport and women's associating their femininity with the delicacy of a butterfly. During the first half of the century, golden treasures of animal figures dangling from necklaces, suspended from earrings, or wound around rings and armlets that were uncovered in excavations of tombs from Antiquity, provided a rich source of ideas. By examining newly exhumed ancient jewels, the Castellani family in Rome were the first to replicate designs identically from the originals. These jewelers were associated with the aristocrat Cavaliere Giampietro Campana, who oversaw excavations at the ancient Etruscan city of Caere. He entrusted them with assembling, cataloguing and restoring the collection. Eventually, the Castellani also used ancient models for original creations, thus spawning an archaeological revival style that was quickly adopted by other prominent jewelers in England and France.

Whereas jewelry in classical times had been worn for its symbolic qualities as well as for decoration, at mid nineteenth century the jewelry of the archaeological revival was desired preeminently for its beauty rather than its association with such animal characteristics as strength or power. Designers accented the predominantly all-gold look of this jewelry with filigree and another goldsmith technique rediscovered from Antiquity, granulation – the fusing of tiny spheres of gold onto a metal base. This style was in sharp contrast to the more formal, courtly jewelry from the neoclassical and First Empire periods when diamonds and colored gemstones dominated the design. The new look must have seemed like a breath of fresh air to the early Victorians, desirous of a change from the somewhat repetitious, staid jewelry designs of the two previous centuries. This became known as the Romantic period, when the distant past held a certain charm – especially artifacts and the life and times of the classical period – and the newly excavated jewels became a link to a bygone era. Since animals had not been present in jewelry since the Renaissance, they seemed natural motifs from the ancients to incorporate in the new designs.

Figurative representations of stags, lions and lionesses, rams and calves found their way into mid-nineteenth century archaeological-style jewelry design, often in the form of the animal's head. Although the ram's head was perhaps one of the most pervasive images, Ernesto Pierret, a Frenchman who relocated to Rome in 1845, preferred the calf's head, encircling it with a laurel wreath as a symbol of victory, using granulation as well as twisting wires to form a rope-like design. His work is not a pastiche of ancient designs. Rather, he borrowed motifs and goldsmith techniques to create imaginative new jewelry using mosaics, enamel work, engraved gemstones, filigree and granulation, which to this day is noted for its high-quality workmanship.

The Campana collection was acquired by Napoleon III. He had it exhibited at Le Palais de l'Industrie in Paris where it excited many French jewelers who, like the Castellani, saw it as a source of inspiration. One of them, the Parisian jeweler, Jules Wièse, eagerly embraced the new style and sought to emulate the appearance of actual antique pieces by replicating the color and surface texture to reproduce the effect of having been buried for a long time. His son, Louis, who took over the firm in 1880, continued to make jewels reminiscent of the archaeological style into the 1890s. His approach to reviving ancient designs was sometimes subtler, as on a link bracelet when he used a lion's head to form the clasp instead of incorporating the entire animal as a dominant motif in the design.

In the second quarter of the nineteenth century, ruins at Herculaneum and Pompeii became fashionable sites to visit. Jewelers, ever on the lookout for fresh sources of inspiration, were quick to adapt mosaics on the floors, ceilings and walls from the ancient villas onto the surface of their designs. One of the most popular images, the Capitoline doves, depicted four birds perched on the rim of a bowl of water, each bird looking in a different direction. Other designs included necklaces with plaques, each with

Two Italian bracelets in the Revivalist style. The first, by Ernesto Pierret, dated 1882, is designed as a sculpted bull's head with a garland around its neck, emerging from a concave medallion decorated with florets and granulated beadwork. The second, c. 1870, is decorated in the centre with a micro-mosaic medallion featuring the dove of peace. *Photo Sotheby's, New York*

a different bird in a variety of poses, and ear pendants featuring mirror images of birds with wings outstretched, often alighting onto a branch. Among the featured images were running stags and reclining dogs within a landscape, most often the King Charles spaniel.

The archaeological style was also evident in Russia, where its inspiration sprang not from Greece or Italy but from within. In 1867, a Scythian treasury was unearthed in the Crimea. In 1882, at the suggestion of Count Sergei Stroganov, the President of the Archaeological Society in St Petersburg, the house of Fabergé made examples based on artifacts uncovered at that site. Work master Erik Kollin created a cast-and-chased bangle bracelet with applied filigree gold wire, each terminal with a band of stylized foliage and a lion's head.

In the third quarter of the century a series of events inspired a fascination for motifs from yet another design source. The opening of the Suez Canal in 1869 and the première in Cairo of Verdi's opera, *Aida*, at about the same time, spawned an almost explosive interest in all things Egyptian. This "craze" lasted until the end of the century when the style was incorporated into Art Nouveau.

It became fashionable to wear Egyptian-style jewels in rich colors, particularly turquoise and gold, with sphinxes, cobras, hawks' heads and scarabs. The ubiquitous scarab from ancient times found its way into the jewelry of such designers in Paris as Eugène Fontenay and Wièse, who created carved turquoise examples that mimic ancient heart amulets. The fascination with Egyptian artifacts continued unabated into the early

This necklace and bracelet, designed by the American T.B. Starr, c. 1903, in the Egyptian revival style, displays enameled gold lotus motif morcels with enameled gold barrel beads, and suspended engraved carnelian scarabs. *Collection High Museum of Art, Atlanta, GA; lent by Virginia Carroll Crawford for the Virginia Carroll Crawford Collection*

twentieth century, spurred on by excavations supported by such institutions as the Brooklyn Museum of Art, the Museum of Fine Arts in Boston and the Metropolitan Museum of Art in New York. Just after the turn of the century, the American firm of Theodore B. Starr created a necklace and bracelet with carved carnelian scarabs, accented with enamel.

Scarabs were not the only insect to intrigue nineteenth-century designers. When the Bonapartes wished to represent the attributes of activity, diligence and hard work on their family crests, they chose the bee, which epitomizes these characteristics, just as the Barberini of Italy had done in the Renaissance. In the nineteenth century, the popularity of insect representations in jewelry also reflected the romantic interest in naturalism.

Once accepted as models, insects became objects of serious study for jewelry designers who readily adapted them into small, yet richly varied formats. A 1904 article in *The Craftsman* explains their appeal: "The singular appearance of insects results not only from the tools and accessories with which they bristle, but also from the immobility of their countenances, from the absence of all expression in their faces. They are knights who have arrayed themselves in their most splendid vestments. Nothing is too beautiful for them: velvet and silk, precious stones and rare metals, superb enamels, laces, brocades, are lavishly used in their garments. Emeralds, rubies and pearls, golds dull and burnished, polished silver, mother-of-pearl mingle, chord, or contrast with one another. They create the sweetest harmonies and the most daring dissonances." (1)

Beginning in the 1860s and lasting for the rest of the century, bejeweled creatures including grasshoppers, wood lice, bees and houseflies (often captured in crystal) were incorporated into brooches, rings, necklaces and lockets. Due in large part to the aesthetic movement in the 1870s and its borrowing of Japanese subject matter, the dragonfly became a dominant image, resurrected later in the Art Nouveau period, while the popularity of the butterfly with its graceful bearing was evident towards the end of the century. The wings of these insects provided a canvas for endless varieties of enameling and the setting of diamonds and gemstones. They were created not only as brooches but also as small lace pins that clung to veils, often worn several at a time. The cicada also made its appearance towards the end of the century; however, instead of setting stones or coloring them with enamel painting, their gossamer wings were executed in *plique-à-jour* enameling, making them seem almost real.

Spiders, the creepy crawlers that make some scream at their sight, became an enthralling insect to capture in precious metal. Their backs could be enameled or set with one or two colored gemstones to show the demarcation of the body, while their multiple legs could be engraved with hair-like lines as on a tarantula or set with diamonds for a more luxurious look. Although, given the threatening countenance of these creatures, the use of spiders seems something of a paradox, in the nineteenth century they were associated with good luck.

Talented designers on both sides of the Atlantic made imaginative jewelry in the guise of insects. Famous houses such as Boucheron and Tiffany & Co. offered

A queen bee pin, designed by Paulding Farnham for Tiffany, c. 1889–93, with ruby eyes, diamond-pavé wings set in gold, rose-cut diamond thorax and a pear-shaped pearl body.
©*Tiffany & Co.*

A gold, enamel and crystal bracelet from the late 1800s featuring a round centre section in whch a jeweled fly is depicted embedded in the crystal. The fly has a ruby and emerald body and diamond wings. The centre is surrounded with a white enamel border and the entire bracelet is decorated with granulated gold balls.
Photo courtesy James Robinson, New York

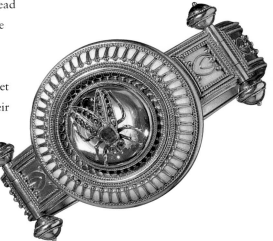

A group of Victorian stick pins depicting various animals popular during the late 1800s and early 1900s. *Photo courtesy J. Mavec & Co., New York*

A Victorian bat brooch in gold set with diamonds in the body and wings, late 1800s. *Photo courtesy Macklowe Gallery, New York*

Sketch of a ring in the shape of a seahorse, late 19th century. *Courtesy Tiffany & Co. Archives*

bejeweled examples; unknown makers in England and France contributed a wide variety of designs, many set with diamonds, colored gemstones or pearls intended for evening wear; and jewelry manufacturers from Newark, New Jersey, produced smaller pieces, suitable for day wear. Bug jewelry enjoyed a forty-year reign of fashion.

Winged creatures from the animal world are not, of course, limited to insects. Nor are they in jewelry. Birds perched on earrings or flying on pendants, necklaces, brooches and châtelaines were crafted in a variety of materials – diamonds, colored gemstones, enameled or in plain gold. In the case of insects, the actual creature was closely depicted, but birds could either portray a generic feathered creature or replicate a real specimen. One of the earliest examples is a pair of pearl and diamond pagoda-shaped ear pendants, probably made in England, with unidentified birds perched on top. In the latter part of the century, an English maker created a demi-parure with a pair of grey-and-brown enameled owls standing within an arched window surrounded by ivy, complemented by a pair of ear pendants, also with owls. Mellerio depicted the peacock with diamonds and enamels and used a feather to create a neck ornament.

In the late 1860s and '70s, traces of Japonisme were evident in all areas of the fine and decorative arts, but especially in jewelry. Several designers were influenced by techniques from this source as well as subject matter taken from Japanese print books, such as Hokusai's *Mangwa*, illustrating animals, insects and birds acting naturally. Asymmetrically arranged oriental compositions were also an inspirational source. In Paris, the designer Alexis Falize captured tropical birds, ducks and roosters flying around lockets, necklaces and châtelaines, decorated by Antoine Tard using the oriental technique of cloisonné enameling. Designers at Tiffany & Co. in New York, probably under the direction of Edward C. Moore, the director of the firm's silver division, produced gold jewelry in the 'Japanesque taste' with applied birds in gold of different colors and platinum.

By the 1890s, the vast array of warm-blooded animals captured in gold and silver included dogs, horses, cats, rabbits, mice, monkeys, bears, bats and lions. Scarf pins became a natural venue for a variety of animal motifs, either carved in gem material or executed in chased gold work and set with diamonds or colored gem stones. Men wore scarf pins in the folds of their linen ties and these, along with cuff links and fob chains with watches, were the acceptable men's accoutrements. Examples of scarf pins with animals range from those with playful and compelling images, such as one with a carved onyx of a cat peering into a goldfish bowl by Boucheron, to a sculpted amethyst dog's head or a labradorite owl. Cuff link offerings included images of dogs' heads or greyhounds curled as if taking a nap. Brooches would feature monkeys dressed like humans or, as in one often repeated example, a diamond-set monkey sitting on a bar from which another monkey hangs from a chain.

The Symbolist movement, with its interest in the macabre and night-time creatures, was responsible for the emergence of the bat as a popular image, usually with outstretched wings enameled or set with diamonds.

Jewelry with reverse intaglios first made their appearance during the 1860s. In these jewels, an animal was carved into the back of a cabochon crystal, painted with the appropriate color for that animal and backed with a piece of mother-of-pearl. In the resulting image, the animal appeared to be floating inside the crystal. Such images included racehorses, sporting animals, dogs, foxes and tigers on brooches, scarf pins and cuff links.

In the 1870s, jewelry set with tiger's claws became fashionable, very likely to commemorate hunting expeditions in India; most of this jewelry was made in Calcutta and sold as souvenirs. In New York, Tiffany & Co produced a brooch with two tiger claws in a mounting enameled with traditional Indian Mogul colors of red, green, turquoise and white. Stylized flowers, leaves and tassels are symmetrically arranged within the over-all design in the Indian fashion. Although Tiffany selected tiger claws simply because they were exotic, in India they were revered as talismans against evil.

As with most fashions, some images were more popular than others. During the late nineteenth century, sea creatures were not as prevalent in jewelry as the snakes, lizards, frogs and turtles that every large and small jewelry house produced in a variety of styles. But the snake, or serpent, had not always been so highly regarded. For more than 1,500 years, the Christian faith had identified its image with the Devil. By the eighteenth century, however, this association had waned due in large measure to the discovery of artifacts from the ancient world. From the neo-classical period towards the end of that century, the snake appeared on chains and necklaces. It achieved prominence as a design source when Queen Victoria wore a coiled snake bracelet for the opening of her first Parliament in 1837. Then, for their betrothal, Prince Albert presented her with an emerald-set serpent ring on which the snake biting its tail, representing eternal love, evoked a symbolism dating to the ancient Greeks. That image, when worn on the wrist of a Victorian lady, was seen as a token of love.

The popularity of the snake as a subject for jewelry resulted from more than its redefined associative meaning and its royal endorsement. The natural shape of this creature offers vast design possibilities. Its long body presented the designer with an endless palette to enamel or set with diamonds, gemstones or pearls to replicate scales. The snake's head can be pavé-set with pearls, diamonds or turquoise and accented with cabochon ruby or garnet eyes. Jewelers in the United States made woven wire bracelets in the form of coiled serpents in silver and gold with the eyes set with rubies and diamonds adorning the head. The fascination for snakes became a craze with the creature slithering around fingers, necks, wrists and upper arms.

Sometime around 1880, a number of brilliant green stones were discovered near the Ural Mountains in Russia. Because of their high brilliance, they were at first believed to be emeralds but were later found to be a particular type of andradite garnet with singular transparency. Since they sparkled like diamonds, they were named demantoid, from *demant*, the Dutch word for diamond. These stones became the natural choice to match the coloration of the backs of lizards, frogs and turtles rendered in large and small

A French monkey brooch, c. 1890, in which the perched monkey is pavé-set with diamonds, ruby eyes and an emerald headpiece; and the suspended monkey is pavé-set with diamonds in the front and sapphires on the reverse. *Photo courtesy Wartski, London*

An amusing clip consisting of a stork formally dressed as a man in a pink and golden topaz and citrine cloak, an aquamarine waistcoat and sapphire trousers. Probably Russian in origin, c. 1880. *Photo courtesy Sandra Cronan, Ltd., London*

jewels, often accented with diamonds or opals. On lizards or salamanders, the stones formed the spine along the back with diamonds on each side, or vice versa.

At mid-century, the Gothic Revival movement spurred an interest in fantasy creatures. Dragons, centaurs and griffins had been part of medieval Christian imagery, representing the demonic world. No longer regarded strictly for that associative quality, jewelers in the nineteenth century saw them as potential distillations of the period's interest in both the past in general and animals in particular. The griffin is a fabulous creature, usually depicted with the head and wings of an eagle and the body of a lion or, sometimes, the tail of a sea creature. Tiffany & Co. in New York and several manufacturing jewelers in

A lion's head brooch, made in England, c. 1830. The flowing mane is made of yellow beryls set in silver-topped gold. The lion's nose and teeth are in white enamel and its tongue in pink enamel. *Collection Neil Lane, Los Angeles. Photo by Tino Hammid*

Newark, New Jersey, captured the beast in gold brooches and scarf pins, often with a pearl or diamond in its mouth.

The centaur is the fabled creature combining the body of a horse and the head and bust of a man. In mythology, it symbolized the savage passions of man and brute force, as well as being an allegory for man divided against himself. Boucheron decorated a tie-pin with a cameo of a centaur with a cupid, made by Rouvillois. The dragon, representing the Devil, was usually portrayed in jewelry with a forked tongue as seen on a pair of enameled ear pendants. Lucien Falize adapted animals into mythical creatures such as the figures on a bracelet each link of which is enameled with bird- and feline-like creatures, none portraying an actual animal.

By the late 1890s, delicate diamond jewelry with swags, ribbons tied in bow knots, tassels, wreaths and garlands became popular. This elegant style of jewelry was known by many names, among them Edwardian or Belle Epoque, and because of the use of garlands it is sometimes called the garland style. Along with these motifs, designers continued to make jewelry in the guise of animals that also reflected this new emphasis. However, instead of employing enameling and interesting colors of gold, these jewels were lavishly set with the stone of the moment, the all-white look of the diamond set into platinum.

Many of the animal motifs from the Victorian period continued into the new century, including dogs, butterflies and snakes, sometimes accented with a bright, contrasting stone. Butterflies were mounted *en tremblant* on hair ornaments with wings and bodies pavé-set with diamonds, or made into brooches, such as one by Boucheron with stylized floral motifs for the wing markings. Téterger in Paris created a butterfly with rubies and citrines set into a frame of tortoise-shell that, even though it dates to 1919, is still designed in the delicate Edwardian style. Snakes were no longer worn for their symbolic associations but for their decorative effects, such as a bracelet from the house of Boucheron with two opposed snake heads with a large diamond in between. In 1915, Cartier created a watch with the black-and-white markings of the panther, an image the firm would use to great advantage later in the century. With a circular dial and oval links, this watch presages the rectilinear style of the Art Deco period.

Throughout the nineteenth century, jewelers took full use of animal imagery in their designs, with representations taken from ancient cultures, the medieval period and the everyday world of insects and domesticated pets. They were made out of gold or carved gem material and set with diamonds, colored gemstones and pearls. It was a fresh new look at nature that enthralled both designers and their clients who enjoyed wearing the latest fashion.

Endnotes
1. Quoted from M.P. Verneuil as translated from the French by Irene Sargent, *The Craftsman*, Vol. 5, No. 6 (March 1904), pp. 567–68.

This brooch by Tiffany & Co., c. 1885, is composed of two actual tiger claws and is decorated with a centre mounting of gold and enamel in the Islamic style. *Photo courtesy Primavera Gallery, New York*

This wristwatch, made in 1915, is one of the first examples of Cartier's trademark panther motif. In platinum and diamonds with onyx spots, the round case frames a square watch face. *Photo Calmels, Chambre, Cohen, Paris*

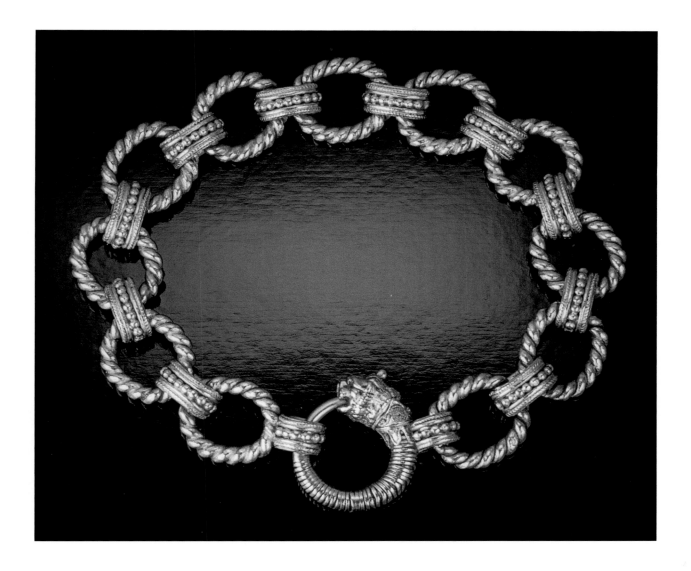

OPPOSITE Gold bangle, terminating in lions' heads, by Carl Fabergé, 1882. This rare example of Scythian treasure was produced by Eric August Kollin and was inspired by recent archaeological finds near Kerch in the Crimea in 1867. *Photo courtesy Wartski, London*

OPPOSITE, CENTRE A brooch made of two chased-gold eagleheads with olivine eyes holding an octagonal peridot in their beaks, and suspending a pear-shaped black peridot pendant. This jewel of 1907 was designed by Lucien Hirtz, made by Espinasse and signed Boucheron. *Collection Boucheron*

ABOVE An 18K gold bracelet with a lion's head clasp by Wièse, c. 1890, in which the rope-motif links are joined to each other with bands of granulation work. *Collection Neil Lane, Los Angeles. Photo by Tino Hammid*

TOP This micro-mosaic and granulated gold pendant featuring a beetle design is probably Italian, late 19th century. *Photo courtesy James Robinson, New York*

ABOVE An 18K gold ring in the Egyptian revival style by Wièse, c. 1880, centering an ancient faience scarab made of turquoise-colored clay. *Collection Neil Lane, Los Angeles. Photo by Tino Hammid*

ABOVE Also in the Egyptian revival style is this engraved turquoise scarab pendant by Eugène Fontenay, c. 1890. The scarab is set in 18K gold granulated work with diamond accents. *Collection Neil Lane, Los Angeles.*

OPPOSITE A mid-19th century archaeological-style necklace with labradorite scarabs and granulation details. *Collection Neil Lane, Los Angeles. Photo © GIA and Tino Hammid*

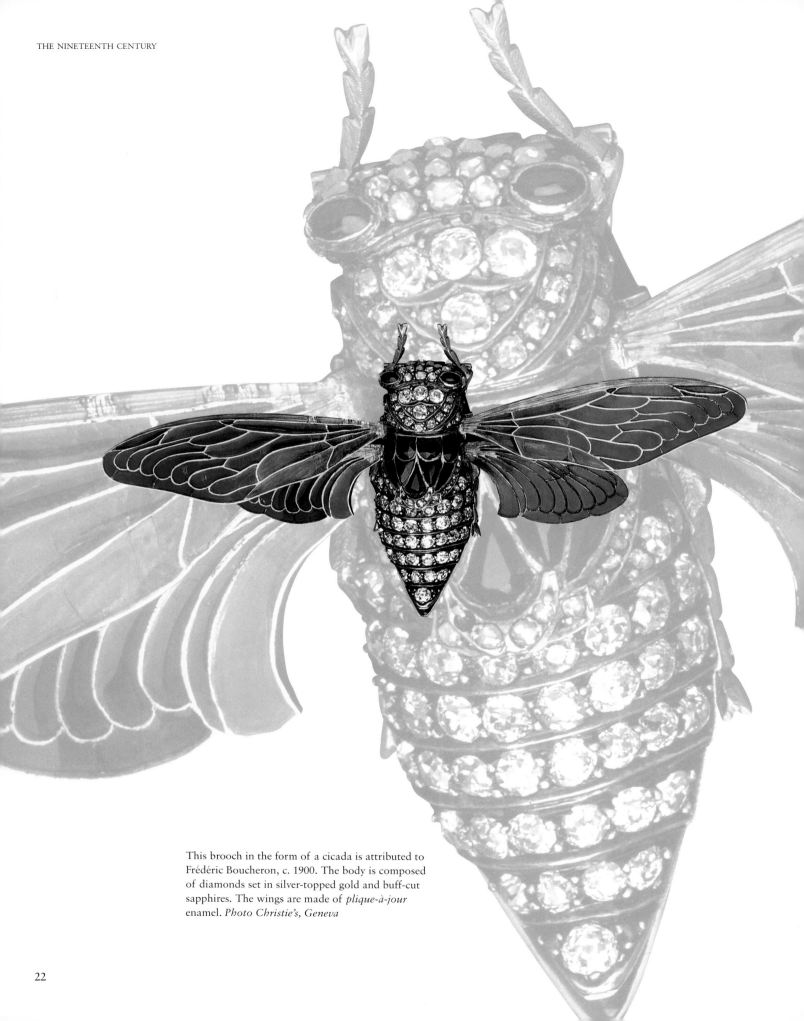

This brooch in the form of a cicada is attributed to Frédéric Boucheron, c. 1900. The body is composed of diamonds set in silver-topped gold and buff-cut sapphires. The wings are made of *plique-à-jour* enamel. *Photo Christie's, Geneva*

Two English grasshopper pins, c. 1905. The one above is made of gold and diamonds with a blue and green opal body. The other one is made of gold, platinum, diamonds and emeralds, and its eyes are cabochon rubies. *Photo courtesy Sandra Cronan Ltd., London*

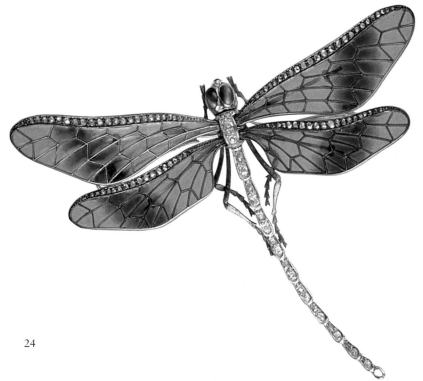

ABOVE This fine Edwardian butterfly of platinum, gold and diamonds is mounted on two tortoise-shell prongs to be worn as a comb. Probably early 1900s American. *Collection Neil Lane, Los Angeles. Photo by Tino Hammid*

LEFT A dragonfly brooch made by Deberghe for Boucheron in 1903. The body is formed by diamonds set in silver-topped gold, while the wings are *plique-à-jour* enamel bordered on the top with rose-cut diamonds. *Collection Boucheron*

TOP An Edwardian-style butterfly clip made
by Boucheron in diamonds set in platinum
and gold, 1907. *Collection Boucheron*

ABOVE This French butterfly brooch, c. 1840,
is made of rose-cut diamonds set in silver-topped
gold. *Collection Neil Lane, Los Angeles.
Photo by Tino Hammid*

FOLLOWING PAGES
LEFT A butterfly brooch made by Téterger, Paris,
1919. The channel-set calibré-cut rubies and citrines
are mounted with 18K gold in wings constructed
of tortoise-shell. The body is made of a tiger's eye
and has cabochon emerald eyes. *Photo courtesy
Firestone & Parson, Boston*

RIGHT The body of this engraved gold and
plique-à-jour butterfly brooch, French, c. 1900, is
made of a cabochon sapphire and a white hardstone.
The eyes are cabochon rubies and the edges of the
wings are engraved with a zigzag and foliate pattern
typical of the period. *Photo courtesy Sandra Cronan,
Ltd., London*

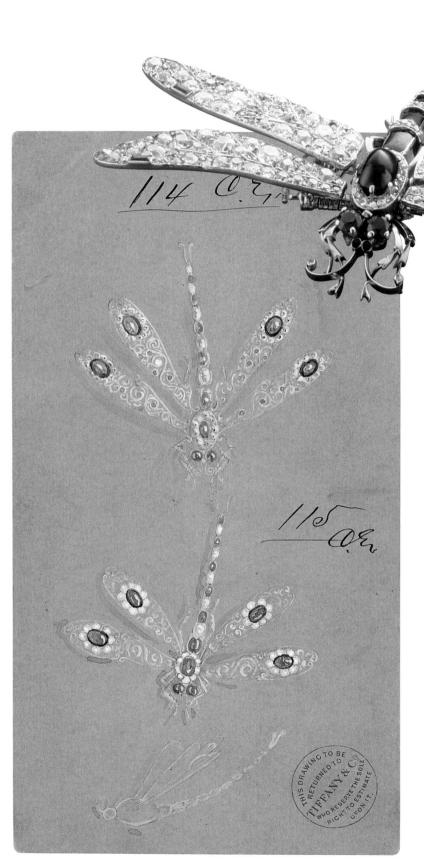

THIS DRAWING TO BE RETURNED TO TIFFANY & Co. WHO RESERVE THE SOLE RIGHT TO ESTIMATE UPON IT.

PREVIOUS PAGES

LEFT An English Victorian spider brooch with diamond-set gold legs and a body made of two large peridots, one emerald-cut and the other octagonal-cut, c. 1870. *Photo courtesy Wartski, London*

RIGHT A brooch in the form of a tarantula by Crane and Theurer, American, c. 1905, features gold, diamonds and enamel. *Private collection. Photo by Robert Weldon*

ABOVE This diamond, sapphire and gold hair ornament in the form of a dragonfly was produced by Tiffany & Co. under the direction of Paulding Farnham, c. 1890. Its lavish setting with precious stones and the *en tremblant* wings reflect the extravagance of the era. *Tiffany & Co. Permanent Collection*

LEFT Sketch of two dragonflies, from the 1893 World's Columbian Exposition in Chicago. *Courtesy Tiffany & Co. Archives*

ABOVE This Victorian gold and enamel demi-parure of owl jewelry, c. 1860, comprises a brooch and a pair of earrings. The brooch portrays two translucent enamel owls sitting in a niche of gold masonry, surrounded by a garland of green enameled ivy. In the earrings, the owls are perched in ivy wreaths. *Photo by David Behl, courtesy Camilla Dietz Bergeron, Ltd., New York*

FOLLOWING PAGES Two pages from the Tiffany & Co. Archives of 19th-century design drawings for jewelry depicting birds. Superimposed on p. 33 is a pair of gold cufflinks in the Japanesque style depicting four different birds, by Tiffany & Co., c. 1890. *Collection Neil Lane, Los Angeles. Photo by Tino Hammid*

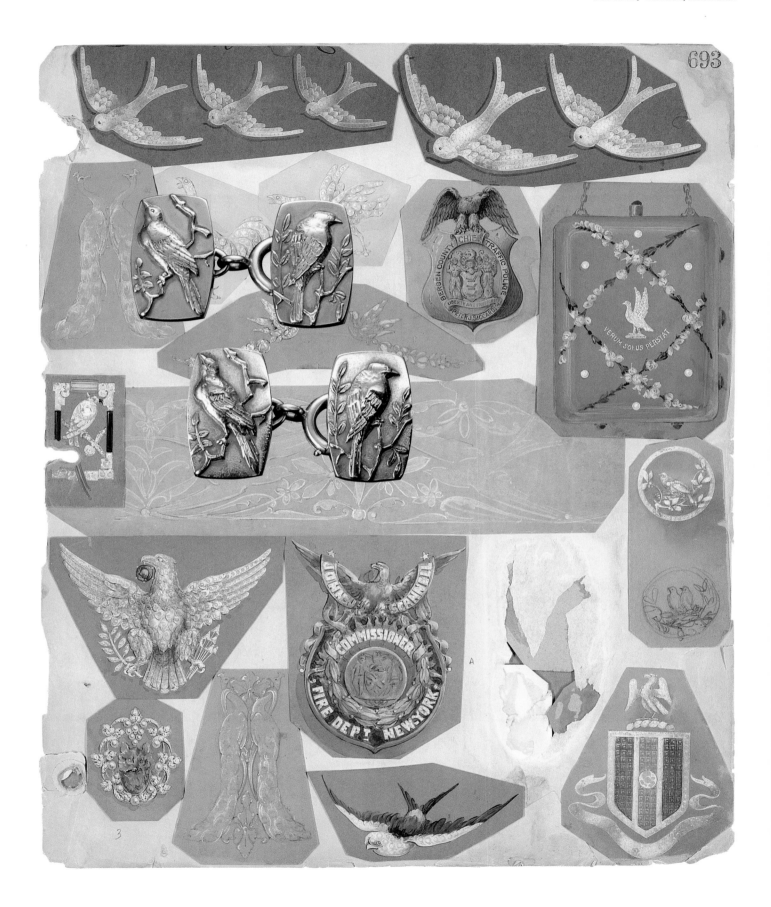

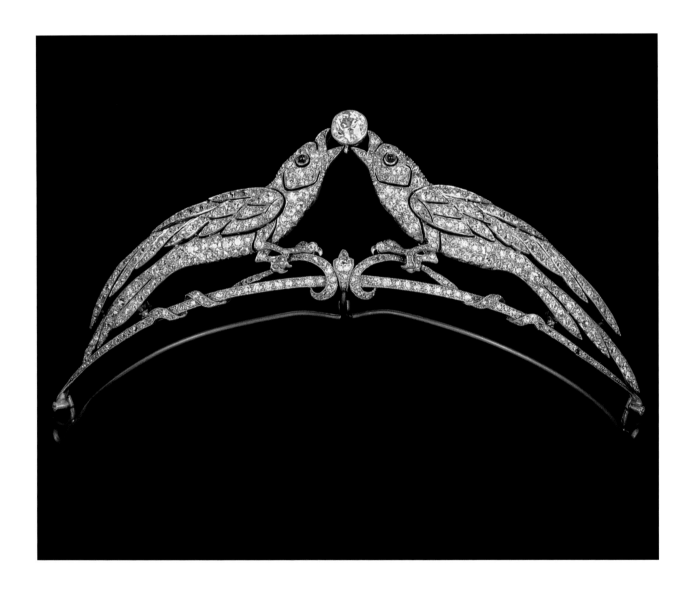

A French platinum and diamond tiara of the
early 1900s, composed of two birds with ruby
eyes holding a large diamond between their
beaks. *Photo courtesy Ulf Breede, Berlin*

These English chandelier earrings, c. 1820, in gold,
silver, pearls, diamonds and rubies, are topped with
a diamond swallow on each. They are 2½ inches long.
Collection Toledo Museum of Art, Toledo, Ohio;
Mr and Mrs George M. Jones, Jr Fund

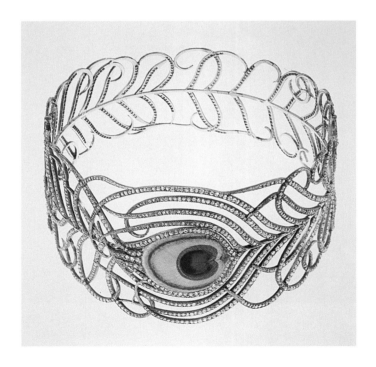

ABOVE A peacock brooch by Mellerio dits Meller, c. 1905, in blue enamel on gold with a spread tail of platinum and diamonds. The eyes on the tail feathers are also enamel on gold. *Private collection. Photo courtesy Mellerio*

LEFT Another Mellerio piece of 1895, a *collier de chien*, or dog collar necklace, with a peacock feather motif in gold, diamonds and enamel. *Collection National Museum of American Art, Smithsonian Institution, Washington. Photo courtesy Mellerio*

OPPOSITE An 18K gold and micro-mosaic lovebird necklace and earrings. Probably Italian, late 19th century. *Photo courtesy James Robinson, New York*

OPPOSITE A grouping of cufflinks from the early 1900s, showing domesticated animals and birds. *Photo courtesy J. Mavec & Co., New York*

ABOVE Four Victorian reverse crystal intaglio pins set in gold and depicting dogs' heads. Originating in the 1860s and remaining popular until the 20th century, the technique involved carving a design into the back of a deep polished rock crystal cabochon. The design was painted and then backed with mother-of-pearl. *Photo courtesy J. Mavec & Co., New York*

RIGHT An Edwardian dog brooch set with rose-cut diamonds and yellow diamonds in silver-topped gold. Signed Cartier, Paris, c. 1910. *Collection Camilla Dietz Bergeron Ltd., New York. Photo by David Behl*

OPPOSITE This spectacular diamond and gold serpent necklace dates from the mid-19th century. It measures 31 inches in length and each articulated bombé segment is set with old-mine-cut diamond clusters. A serpent in the form of a circle with its tail in its mouth was a symbol of eternity. *Photo Christie's New York*

RIGHT An articulated snake necklace of the late 19th century in gold and set with pearls representing the scales of the body. The head is set with small pearls and accented with one ruby and one emerald eye outlined with diamonds. *Photo courtesy Ulf Breede, Berlin*

This is an English salamander brooch in gold
set with opals, demantoid garnets and diamonds,
c. 1840. *Collection Silver & Co., London.*
Photo courtesy Wartski, London

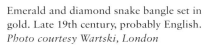

Emerald and diamond snake bangle set in gold. Late 19th century, probably English.
Photo courtesy Wartski, London

pierres de couleurs seulement sur ceux ...
Gargf les yeux de ceux d'or en rubis

OPPOSITE A page of late 19th-century design drawings from Mellerio for unusual link bracelets, each link being a coiled snake.

ABOVE A gold and diamond brooch, c. 1890, in the form of a snake guarding a large red tourmaline. This jewel was given by King Edward VII to his mistress, Mrs Keppel. *Photo courtesy Wartski, London*

RIGHT This articulated bracelet from Boucheron, 1907, shows two diamond snakes hugging a 2-carat round diamond. Set in white gold, the snakes' heads are each pear-shaped diamonds accented by calibré-cut emeralds and sapphires with ruby eyes. *Photo Calmels, Chambre, Cohen, Paris*

BELOW RIGHT A flexible platinum and diamond snake bracelet, American, c. 1917. The head is a pear-shaped diamond with cabochon ruby eyes, and the body is accented with diamond baguettes and calibré-cut emeralds. When closed, the snake appears to coil around itself. *Collection Neil Lane, Los Angeles. Photo by Tino Hammid*

OPPOSITE A page of late 19th-century design drawings of jewelry from the Tiffany & Co. Archives depicting griffins and fantasy animals. Superimposed over this is one of a pair of Victorian gold and enamel pendant earrings with dragons painted on white enamel and insects on the earpieces. The reverse side is enameled with a foliate motif and set with pearls, rubies and diamonds on pink enamel. *Photo courtesy James Robinson, New York.* Below is a cameo tie pin made for Boucheron by Rouvillois in 1877, which depicts a centaur and a cupid in a blue and gold enamel setting. *Collection Boucheron*

ABOVE Two chimeras and the initial "M" appear on this Mellerio brooch, made of gold, enamel, silver-topped gold and diamonds, c. 1875. *Photo courtesy Mellerio*

RIGHT A Mellerio hair ornament of 1896 features a chimera in silver, gold and enamel. *Photo courtesy Mellerio*

OPPOSITE This is a gold and enamel bracelet in the medieval taste by Lucien Falize, c. 1880. Each of the articulated segments portrays a mythological creature in alternating red and blue enamel. *Photo courtesy Ulf Breede, Berlin*

ABOVE Two châtelaines by Alexis Falize, c. 1869, in gold and cloisonné enamel. The one on the left shows a rooster, a hen and chicks pecking at feed on a white enamel ground. In the other one two exotic birds are perched on a tropical flowering tree. *Photos courtesy Wartski, London*

RIGHT This locket by Alexis Falize, c. 1869, in gold and cloisonné enamel depicts a dragonfly eating pollen from a flower. *Photo courtesy Wartski, London*

ABOVE LEFT A turtle brooch in gold, diamonds and demantoid garnets made by Alfred Menu, French, c. 1900. *Photo courtesy Sandra Cronan, Ltd., London*

ABOVE RIGHT A diamond turtle from the late 1800s. *Photo courtesy Sandra Cronan, Ltd., London*

BELOW This late 19th-century crab pin in silver-topped gold, gold and platinum, with a body centering a cushion-cut garnet surrounded by old-mine-cut diamonds, is probably English in origin. *Private collection. Photo © GIA and Tino Hammid*

A pair of early 20th-century crab clips in platinum, gold and diamonds. The centre stones are rose-cut diamonds. *Private collection. Photo © GIA and Tino Hammid*

Chapter 2

Art Nouveau
Unrestrained Creativity – New Forms and Materials

Towards the end of the nineteenth century, the enthusiasm for the new, which had so energized and revolutionized the jewelry world, was running its course. A group of designers in France conceived of a totally new way to create jewelry, not dependent upon traditions from the past but focused on art itself. This innovative movement, which became known as Art Nouveau – taking its name from the gallery *L'Art Nouveau* that Siegfried Bing opened in Paris on December 26, 1895 – introduced a new vocabulary into the repertoire of jewelry, in terms of both design and techniques. Its undisputed leader was René Lalique, who created pieces that defied the conventions of jewelry forms, becoming art more than (wearable) jewels. Other proponents of the style included Henri Vever, Lucien Gaillard and Georges Fouquet in France, Philippe Wolfers in Belgium and Louis Comfort Tiffany in the United States. The Art Nouveau style in jewelry did not evolve in a vacuum but co-existed with the Edwardian style that was more an outgrowth of nineteenth-century designs than a look to the future.

During the nineteenth century, animals in jewelry were, for the most part, portrayed naturalistically. Some designers even went so far as to bring live specimens into the studio so as to replicate the actual animal in painstaking detail. In contrast, Art Nouveau is characterized by a free-flowing 'whiplash' line that expresses movement, passion and vitality as it connects the various components of the design. Everything teems with an energy which seems to flow out of the compositions. Typical Art Nouveau tableaux depicting animal themes feature wriggling marine life, preening birds, writhing reptiles and metamorphosing insects.

Insects became the prevalent models in Art Nouveau jewelry, with designers transforming them into fantasy creatures that were at the same time sensuously appealing and startling in their portrayal. Among the most often depicted subjects were the butterfly and the dragonfly, sometimes created in new materials such as horn and often shown metamorphosing into a woman. Although René Lalique took the latter idea to an extreme in a corsage ornament of a hybrid dragonfly, other designers created less macabre figures. Louis Comfort Tiffany depicted a more realistic example with black opals for the body and demantoid garnets between platinum filigree wings. Platinum had become acceptable as a metal for jewelry beginning about 1895, but was not universally employed until the first decade of the twentieth century. On the Tiffany piece, the webbings on the wings are demarcated with platinum without any coloration.

In real life, insect wings are thin and transparent, like cellophane, their strength provided by a framework of small tubular veins. In jeweled insects, wing veins rendered in gold provide cell walls to which transparent enameling adheres. After firing, the backing is removed, and when held to the light the resulting gossamer effect is reminiscent of a real wing. Known as *plique-à-jour* enameling, this technique was used to great advantage by Art Nouveau jewelers. Philippe Wolfers created a moth with wings in *plique-à-jour* enameling whose execution in graduated tints is so fine that it is difficult to determine where one color begins and the next ends.

A butterfly emerging from a caterpillar came to epitomize the act of metamorphosis during the Art Nouveau period. In jewelry, the butterfly would be represented with the body of a woman while retaining its wings. This reinterpretation became a graphical metaphor for the changing role of women in society as a result of the suffragette movement. The brooch by Whiteside & Blank from Newark, New Jersey depicts such a metaphor. The woman's diaphanous gown is a translucent lime green enamel, a color reiterated in the upper wings with *plique-à-jour* enameled sections. Butterflies were not always captured in transitional states. Henri Vever depicted a more stylized version in diamonds on a hair comb, an accessory for the lady who wore her hair swept up on the back of her head.

This style is also known for its use of non-traditional jewelry material, such as the humble horn, from which jewelers contrived to create works of art. Horn exhibits a natural surface sheen and, when heated, it can be worked into different shapes. Lucien Gaillard favored horn for his designs, often inspired by the simplicity of Japanese designs. The wings on a pair of moths, carved from thin horn material, are joined along one edge in a symmetrical arrangement, their panels overlapping to give depth and shadowing. The markings on the wings are enameled in simple circular patterns.

Bees were also a favorite theme of Art Nouveau jewelers, but instead of depicting them by themselves as in typical Victorian designs, both Gaillard and Lalique incorporated them as part of a tableau, alighting on plants. The Gaillard bees hover over flowers, drawing nectar from the pistil, while Lalique's bees nibble on sheaves of wheat. The beetle is another insect inherited from the Victorian period; however, instead of giving it connotations associated with ancient Egypt, Louis Comfort Tiffany produced an entire line of such jewelry, made out of favrile glass which simulates the iridescence of the insect.

In the avian world, vultures represented a sinister aspect of Art Nouveau while owls and bats were reminders of the eerie night. The swan, a symbol of pride as well as metamorphosis, swam within jewels, its long neck

Designed by Louis Comfort Tiffany, this dragonfly brooch is made of black opals and demantoid garnets set in gold, and the wings are constructed of platinum filigree veins. It was exhibited at the St. Louis exhibition in 1904. *Tiffany Permanent Collection*

A butterfly in the shape of a woman was a typical Art Nouveau notion. This example, made by Whiteside and Blank, c. 1900, is composed of gold, diamonds, enamel and *plique-à-jour*. *Collection of the Newark Museum, Purchase 1993, The Millicent Fenwick Fund*

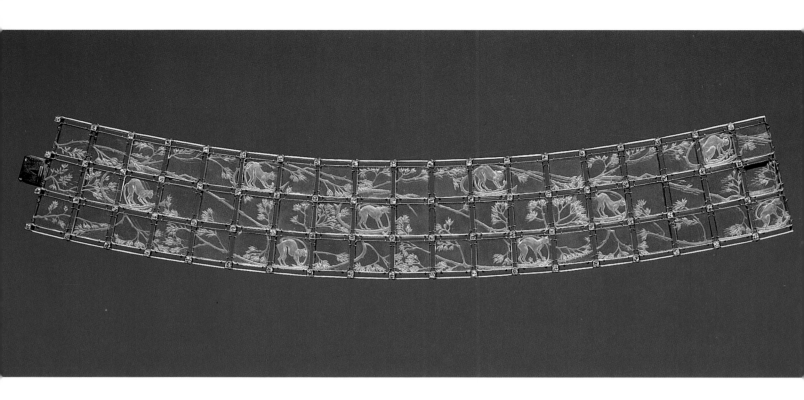

Cats climbing in tree branches are depicted in this necklace of gold, rock crystal and diamonds created by René Lalique, 1906–08. *Photo Calouste Gulbenkian Museum, Lisbon*

allowing the designer to develop a sinuous line, as seen in the pendant Lalique created for Queen Alexandra of Great Britain. But the bird that reigned supreme during these years was the peacock, combining its natural beauty with the fantasy of the period while signifying the underlying narcissism of Art Nouveau. It is generally depicted either displaying or folding up its tail, mimicking the solar drama of the earth revolving about the sun (or vice versa, as it was thought for many centuries). The natural sheen of the peacock's feathers offered the jeweler endless possibilities for displaying their beauty in either translucent, matte or *plique-à-jour* enameling while finishing their 'eyes' with foiled enamel, moonstones or opals. Vever displayed the proud bird against a background of cut opal with its tail feathers streaming downward. René Foy's two peacocks turn their heads backward to form loops for the chain. In Lalique's piece, tail feathers encircle the neck and head, their eyes rendered in heart-shaped moonstones. The body of Gautrait's majestic peacock occupies the center of the pendant, its head turned to one side, the tail feathers fanned behind in *champlevé* and *plique-à-jour* enamel with opal eyes.

Mammals are not common in Art Nouveau jewelry, as their visages were considered not readily adaptable to the style. However, Lalique created a few examples, purchased by his patron, Calouste Gulbenkian, and now housed in the museum in Lisbon that bears his name. They include a corsage ornament with knights on horseback; hair combs with bears or dogs; and a neck ornament with cats in different poses, their tails forming a sinuous line that wraps part way around their bodies. In the Walters Art Museum, Baltimore, the savagery of the tiger is shown on a necklace, which consists of plaques with striding tigers with claws on each side, alternating with feline incisor teeth.

Aquatic creatures were infrequent images in nineteenth-century jewelry design. However, the underwater world with its teeming life and undulating movement could not but appeal to Art Nouveau jewelry designers, eager for a new source to exploit the essence of the style. Lalique depicted fish life in both precious materials and in glass. On one of his corsage ornaments, fish are formed out of molded glass, enameled in light and dark blue to replicate the coloring of the fish. Sea horses facing each other across the water are depicted on a brooch with *plique-à-jour* enamel contained within gold wave-like cells mimicking the movement of the sea with opals forming bubbles. Lalique also captured frogs on a dog collar, some shown skimming along on top of the water while one surreally clasps onto the hat of a woman.

A ring in the shape of a dragonfly with *plique-à-jour* enamel designed by Lucien Gaillard, c. 1900. The insect's body is decorated with black *champlevé* enamel and faceted emeralds. The wings, which form the ring, are decorated with opalescent foiled *plique-à-jour*. *Photo courtesy Ulf Breede, Berlin*

Instead of depicting aquatic life within a tableau, Georges Fouquet created a fantasy fish out of an abalone pearl shell body with *plique-à-jour* fins and tail, the result of his collaboration with the Czech graphic artist, Alphonse Mucha. They also joined forces on a hand ornament for Sarah Bernhardt that is at once strikingly beautiful and shocking, featuring a coiled snake motif reminiscent of ancient Greek prototypes as well as examples from the Victorian period. Its association with sexuality and its connotations of evil seemed appropriate for Bernhardt who played such characters as Medea and Cleopatra. Lalique, on one of his jewels, turned the snake into a threatening creature coiled around the tails of eight others, each with its mouth gaping as if to bite its prey. This piece epitomizes the period's interest in snakes as the living embodiment of the whiplash line.

Equally impressive is another sea serpent corsage ornament, designed by Charles Desrosiers for Georges Fouquet. The enameled serpent's body is formed in a dramatic curvilinear design and on each side of the head are exquisitely crafted *plique-à-jour* wings. The strong movement of the line on the serpent is softened by tapering seaweed motifs supporting a natural pearl.

By 1910, the Art Nouveau style in jewelry had become debased by too many poor imitators, impelling Lalique to discontinue making jewelry in precious materials and turning his attention instead to glass making. Within a short period of time, a new style emerged, based on rectilinear design, that was diametrically opposed to the premises of Art Nouveau.

This ring of gold-encrusted steel with a bat pattern was made in 1907 by Provost-Blondel for Boucheron. *Collection Boucheron*

OPPOSITE A bumble bee hair comb made by René Lalique, c. 1900, in carved and painted horn, in the form of two sheaves of wheat, each applied with an insect. *Photo courtesy Ulf Breede, Berlin*

ABOVE A graceful moth pendant designed by Lucien Gaillard, c. 1900, in carved horn with 18K gold enamel and faceted citrines. *Photo © Historical Design, New York*

ABOVE This elaborate gold and enamel corsage
ornament by Lalique, 1898–99, shows nine intertwined
snakes. *Photo Calouste Gulbenkian Museum, Lisbon*

OPPOSITE A corsage ornament by Georges Fouquet,
1902, in the form of a winged sea monster with a body
in cloisonné enamel and fins and tail in *plique-à-jour*.
The top of the snake's head is a lozenge-shaped emerald
bordered with calibré-cut emeralds, perched on a
stylized algae motif in gold, rose-colored baroque
pearls and diamonds. *Private collection*

TOP LEFT An English diamond and enamel bat brooch, c. 1900. The body is pavé-set diamonds in silver-topped gold with ruby eyes and *plique-à-jour* wings. *Photo courtesy Wartski, London*

TOP RIGHT A French butterfly brooch, c. 1900, in *plique-à-jour* enamel set with opals and diamonds. *The Anderson Collection of Art Nouveau, University of East Anglia, Norwich*

ABOVE A belt buckle by Lalique, c. 1903–04, made of gold and *plique-à-jour* enamel with an opal in the centre set with sapphires. *The Anderson Collection of Art Nouveau, University of East Anglia, Norwich*

A dragonfly brooch attributed to Louis Aucoc, c. 1900.
The body is made of gold accented with cabochon ruby
eyes, and the tail, in *plique-à-jour* enamel, is shaded
from deep blue to turquoise. The outstretched wings
are made of carved horn edged with rose-cut diamonds
and pierced with small areas of enamel.
Photo Sotheby's, London

ABOVE This moth brooch by the Belgian jeweler Philippe Wolfers, c. 1900, features gold, rubies, diamonds, pearls and *plique-à-jour* enamel. *Private collection*

OPPOSITE A dramatic gold, enamel, opal and diamond hand ornament in the form of a winged serpent with enameled scales on the body, which forms the bracelet coiling up the arm. The head, decorated with an opal mosaic and cabochon opal eyes, is designed to rest on top of the hand. The serpent bites on a ring from which gold chains are suspended, which attach to a smaller winged serpent ring. This jewel, designed in Paris in 1899 by Alphonse Mucha, the most celebrated decorative artist of his day, was executed by Georges Fouquet for Sarah Bernhardt. *Photo Christie's, Geneva*

OPPOSITE A comb in the form of an owl made by Vever in 1900. The constituents of the jewel are horn, gold, *plique-à-jour* enamel, cabochon emeralds (for the eyes) and rose-cut diamonds. *Musée des Arts Décoratifs, Paris. Photo L. Sully-Jaulmes*

RIGHT This belt buckle of gold, enamel and cabochon carnelians in the form of a peacock was designed in 1900 by Lucien Grasset and executed by Vever. *Musée des Arts Décoratifs, Paris. Photo Georges Fessy*

BELOW Four frosted glass owls sit on a pine branch in this gold and enamel link bracelet by René Lalique, c. 1900. Chalcedony eggs are held in claws at the top and bottom of each panel. *Photo Calouste Gulbenkian Museum, Lisbon*

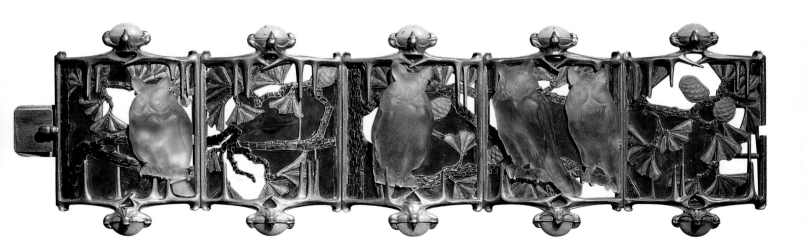

TOP LEFT A pendant by René Foy, c. 1900–02, on which two green enamel peacocks flank the head of a third peacock surrounded by a network of stylized peacock feathers, from which a pearl is suspended. *Photo courtesy Macklowe Gallery, New York*

TOP RIGHT A Lalique pendant in gold, white enamel and *plique-à-jour* enamel in the form of a stylized swan. The centre of the piece depicts two swans swimming in a body of water, represented by wavy gold lines. This jewel belonged to Queen Alexandra of Great Britain and was illustrated in *L'Art Décoratif* in 1902. *Photo courtesy Ulf Breede, Berlin*

ABOVE LEFT A peacock pendant designed by L. Gautrait, c. 1900. The bird's *plique-à-jour* enameled wings, made of cast and chased gold, are accented with opals representing the feathers, while an opal hangs below. *Photo courtesy Ulf Breede, Berlin*

ABOVE RIGHT In this pendant by Vever, c. 1900, the peacock is perched on a gold floral branch. The blue enamel bird is set against an opal background surrounded by diamond flowers set in silver-topped gold. The enameled tail feathers cascade down the length of the piece. *Photo courtesy Ulf Breede, Berlin*

This necklace designed by Louis Comfort Tiffany,
c. 1910, is made of favrile glass beetles set in gold
and connected by a gold chain and gold bead links.
*Collection of Louis Comfort Tiffany Garden
Mueum, Matsue, Japan. Photo Townsend*

A massive necklace by Lalique, 1903–04, in which
striding tigers carved in horn alternate with pointed
tortoise-shell-shaped feline incisors. Beneath each
tiger is a polished round triangle of brown agate
mounted in gold with a claw extending from each
side of the medallion. Henry Walters bought this
unique necklace at the St. Louis World's Fair of
1904. *Collection The Walters Art Museum,
Baltimore, Maryland*

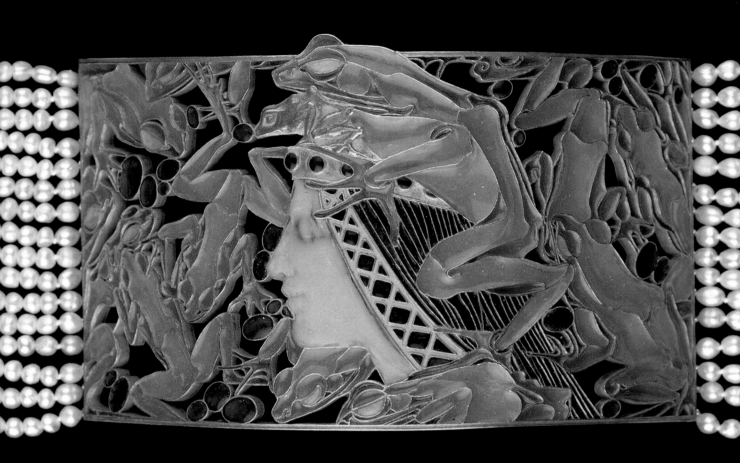

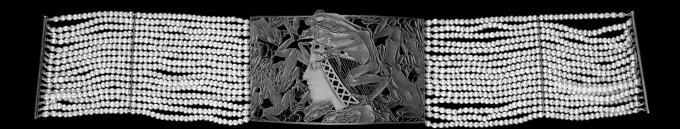

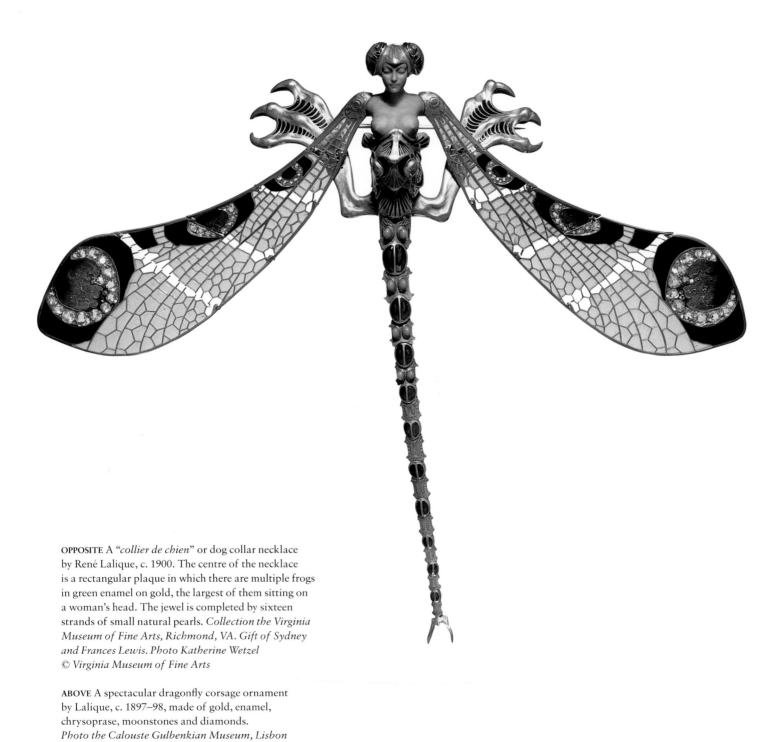

OPPOSITE A "*collier de chien*" or dog collar necklace
by René Lalique, c. 1900. The centre of the necklace
is a rectangular plaque in which there are multiple frogs
in green enamel on gold, the largest of them sitting on
a woman's head. The jewel is completed by sixteen
strands of small natural pearls. *Collection the Virginia
Museum of Fine Arts, Richmond, VA. Gift of Sydney
and Frances Lewis. Photo Katherine Wetzel
© Virginia Museum of Fine Arts*

ABOVE A spectacular dragonfly corsage ornament
by Lalique, c. 1897–98, made of gold, enamel,
chrysoprase, moonstones and diamonds.
Photo the Calouste Gulbenkian Museum, Lisbon

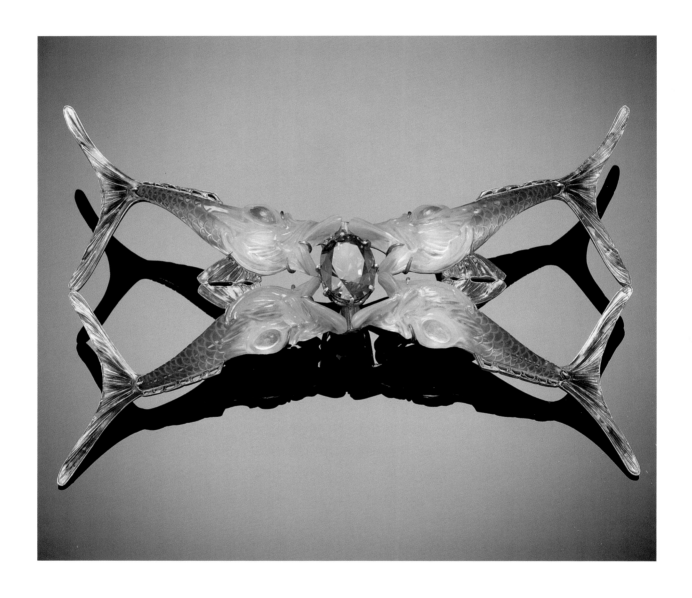

This Lalique corsage ornament, c. 1900,
shows four opalescent enameled fish
surrounding a faceted sapphire set
in gold. *Photo Sotheby's, Geneva*

ABOVE Corsage ornament in the form of a fish, made by Georges Fouquet in 1901. The body of the fish is a large abalone baroque pearl with gold framed *plique-à-jour* enamel fins and tail. A four-chain châtelaine of items made of pearls, turquoise and gold is suspended from the fish's mouth. *Photo Christie's, Geneva*

RIGHT A Lalique brooch, c. 1902–05, in which two enamel seahorses mirror each other across a sea of pink and green *plique-à-jour* enamel with gold waves and foiled inclusions. Opal bubbles rise from the triangular stone. A pearl is suspended from the seabed. *Collection of the Virginia Museum of Art, Richmond, VA. The Sydney and Frances Lewis Art Nouveau Fund. Photo Katherine Wetzel © Virginia Musum of Fine Arts*

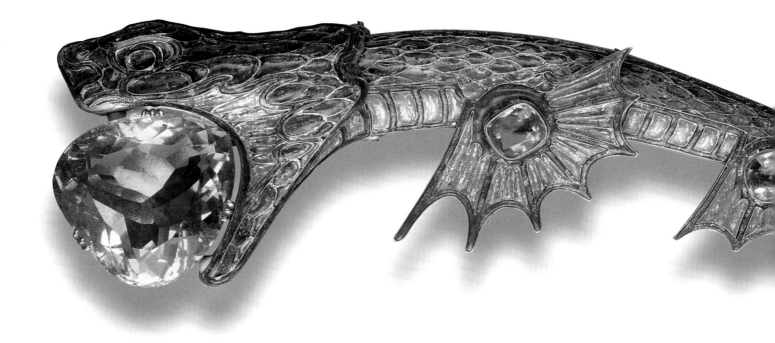

This extraordinary articulated dragon brooch
made of enamel on gold, set with aquamarines,
is believed to be the work of Etienne Tourette,
c. 1903. *Photo courtesy N. Manoukian, Paris*

Chapter 3

Art Deco
Geometricized Designs and Foreign Influences

The Art Nouveau movement freed jewelry design from outmoded influences of the nineteenth century. The advent of Art Deco took this evolution a step further, affirming the virtues of simple geometrical forms and brilliant color schemes. The style which eventually became known as Art Deco traces its origins to the period before World War I. Performances of Serge Diaghilev's Ballets Russes in Paris in 1909 and in the United States in 1916 brought bright colors into an arguably drab world of fashion. In the fine arts, the Cubist movement had been launched in 1907 with Pablo Picasso's *Demoiselles d'Avignon*, in which the human figure was divided into flat, overlapping configurations. In 1909, the Italian poet, Marinetti, published the Futurist Manifesto which heralded the machine, urban life and speed as the pictorial expressions of a new reality. The Dutch De Stijl painter, Piet Mondrian, carried Cubism further, into Neo-plasticism, freeing forms through abstraction from any suggestion of reality.

This new way of conceiving art was quickly assimilated by leading jewelers whose designs became rectilinear – with square, rectangular and triangular shapes, in addition to the circle, as basic elements. These designers replaced traditional jewelry techniques of enameling and chasing with a modern palette, using new diamond cuts and contrasting colored semi-precious gemstones with precious ones to achieve striking chromatic effects. Amethysts, aquamarine, lapis lazuli, jade, coral, topaz, turquoise, onyx and rock crystal were juxtaposed with diamonds and emeralds. Surface treatment was given added interest with faceted stones next to flat or cabochon stones and an array of new diamond cuts, such as baguette, trapezium, table and square, all providing the designs with rectilinearity. Within this new decorative vocabulary, the enameling color palette consists primarily of strong hues of red, black and white. For the most part a French movement, the new style numbered among its major proponents Cartier, Van Cleef & Arpels, Boucheron, Mauboussin and Janesich.

Animal figures had reigned supreme for a hundred years, with great attention to detail aimed at achieving either naturalistic likeness or explicit symbolic or dream-like imagery. In Art Deco, figures become abstracted into flat, two-dimensional forms bearing a likeness to their original models but rendered in a new vernacular. Formerly represented as charming or menacing, symbolic or sentimental, animals were now depicted in simpler formats that emphasize overall design over detailed content.

The discovery of Tutankhamen's tomb by Howard Carter in 1922 became another major factor contributing to the direction taken by Art Deco jewelry design. This event launched another veritable Egyptian craze in the art world. Cartier incorporated ancient faience beetles into some designs, often replicating ancient Egyptian funerary ornaments. Another source of inspiration was offered by the clean lines in hieroglyphic calligraphy; these were readily reinterpreted according to the linear concepts of Art Deco. Van Cleef & Arpels, among others, introduced stylized pharaonic motifs into a series of bracelets, shoulder clips and brooches. On a flexible pictorial bracelet, images associated with the dead are beautifully portrayed. Two images of Anubis, the god of the dead shown in canine form, flank a representation of a Western version of Ba-bird, a combination of human head on a falcon's body which, on this bracelet, is depicted as a woman with outstretched wings. Janesich interpreted the subject on a bracelet with stylized sphinxes. On both these bracelets, the actual designs are executed with calibré-cut rubies, emeralds and sapphires, contrasted with the starkness of onyx with an all-white background of diamonds. The Eyptian influence is also evident on a pendant with an ibis whose neck is in the shape of a Celtic interlace, atop an upside-down stylized lotus.

The most pervasive animal image in jewelry of this period is that of a bird, its triangular-shaped wings and tail feathers providing an area to be filled in with gemstones cut in modern shapes. In the first half of the 1920s, pavé-set circular-cut diamonds made up the bodies, feathers and tail feathers of birds. By mid-decade, these were augmented with rectilinear-shaped stones. A crane brooch by Janesich depicts the pavé-set bird flying with its wings flapping downward, one wing set with triangular-cut diamonds. This brooch, featuring onyx trimming on one side of each wing and on the tail feathers, is also characteristic of the black-and-white look popular by the mid-1920s. Another example of this style is a clip by Van Cleef & Arpels in the guise of a swallow made out of baguette diamonds for the body, wings and tail feathers and a pear-shaped diamond head. Contrast is provided by a shaped piece of onyx for the center of the body, base of the tail feathers and beak. Louis Aucoc, better known for his Art Nouveau jewelry, designed a brooch with a stylized bird, trimmed in black enamel in the place of onyx and

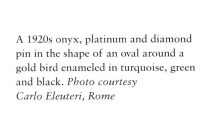

A 1920s onyx, platinum and diamond pin in the shape of an oval around a gold bird enameled in turquoise, green and black. *Photo courtesy Carlo Eleuteri, Rome*

emeralds. Perhaps the most animated of the bird depictions is a jabot pin by Janesich with fighting cocks on each end, one flying up in the air as if about to attack the other. It is constructed not in a flat format but three-dimensionally with wings jutting out from the bodies. A sense of action is also achieved on a flexible bracelet by the American firm, Oscar Heyman & Brothers, on which swooping tropical birds fly amid a floral background. It is set with calibré-cut rubies, emeralds and sapphires to provide a polychrome palette and its surface treatment is in contrast to the circular-cut diamonds.

Black-and-white colorations were also evident on jewelry with furry animals. Cartier and Mauboussin created tiger brooches in which onyx delineated the stripes amid circular-cut diamonds, thus achieving a realistic effect. Cartier began their series of panther jewelry with the use of onyx for the spots, while the American maker, Udall & Ballou, designed a running dog with half of its body enameled black. The dog, running at top speed with its front legs tucked between its back legs, brings to mind the Futurist painting by Giacomo Balla, *Dynamism of a Dog on a Leash*, in which the dog's legs and tail are shown in rapid motion. Cartier created a pair of cuff links with black enameled dogs' heads against a diamond-set ground, and Boucheron, in their sporting jewelry, used enamel for the jockey's silk with his horse in diamonds. Scarf pins by Boucheron also followed the animal theme with diamond-set horses, dogs, rabbits, fish and birds.

The reptilian world was represented in Art Deco jewelry by turtles and snakes, pictorially depicted in a flat, two-dimensional manner. On a jabot pin, a snake is rendered in diamonds and calibré-cut sapphires with its coiled body at one end and its tail at the other.

The running dog designed by Udall & Ballou, c. 1920. *Photo © 2000 Historical Design, Inc., New York*

This racehorse brooch in pavé diamonds with a jockey in enamel was made for Boucheron by Atelier Canivé in 1928. *Photo Boucheron Archives*

ABOVE A 1929 design from the Mauboussin Archives for a swan brooch in diamonds, calibré-cut rubies and onyx

ABOVE LEFT In this cutting from a 1927 article in *L'Illustration* entitled "Le Bijou Moderne", written by Henri Clouzot, curator at the Musée Galliera in Paris, the lozenge-shaped brooch in platinum, diamonds and emerald by Louis Aucoc features a stylized bird outlined in black enamel. The brooch on the right is a jewel in the shape of a turtle by Mauboussin, Paris, made of the same materials.

The chimera is a monster from Greek mythology having several heads, the fore-parts of a lion, the middle section of a goat, and the rear a dragon. It became a popular motif during the Art Deco period. Designers at Cartier drastically changed its appearance, basing their interpretation on Oriental prototypes, especially the Indian sea monster, the *makara*, to carve the terminals on a bangle consisting of two chimera heads touching each other with their jaws open. In the original model, the heads were of coral with two carved spherical emeralds between. By the end of the 1920s, the heads had become streamlined, set with diamonds, and the spheres had been eliminated. The firm continued to use this simplified design for the next several decades.

By 1930, the Art Deco style had waned. The flat, two-dimensional style gave way to a sculptural style using softer geometrical shapes. Animal figures evolved toward a more realistic appearance. Bright, strong colors became muted. With the change in the economic climate following the stock market crash in October 1929, the jewelry business changed. Only those who were able to create a new look survived.

ABOVE A 1920s design from the Mauboussin Archives for a terrier brooch in platinum, onyx and diamonds.

LEFT Two pairs of 1920s Art Deco cufflinks by Cartier, Paris, portraying dogs' heads in black enamel on white gold, silhouetted by rose-cut diamonds. These were probably a special commission to memorialize someone's favourite pets. *Photo courtesy S.J. Phillips, London*

An impressive "Flying Scarab" brooch in the Egyptian revival style by Cartier, London, 1925. The ancient Egyptian blue faience scarab is studded with small emerald and ruby cabochons and flanked by curved spread wings, channel-set with buff-cut citrines, rubies and emeralds alternating with pavé diamonds and onyx rows. *Collection Art of Cartier. Photo Nick Welch © Cartier*

A brooch in the form of a duck made by Mauboussin in platinum, diamonds and calibré-cut sapphires, rubies, emeralds and onyx. *Photo Christie's, New York* Below it is a design for the brooch in a 1925 Mauboussin catalogue. *Mauboussin Archives*

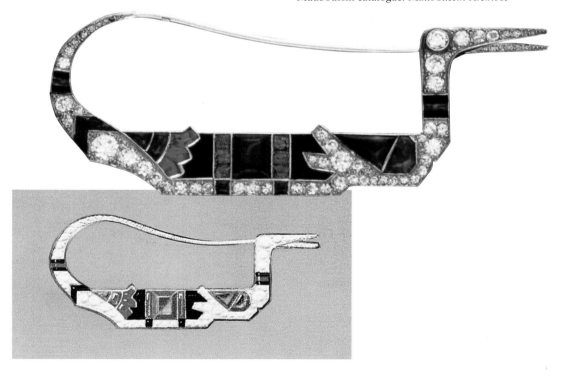

This Egyptian revival bracelet from Van Cleef
& Arpels, Paris, c. 1925, is decorated with
buff-cut ruby scarabs as well as human figures
in buff-cut rubies, emeralds, sapphires and onyx.
Photo Antiquorum, New York

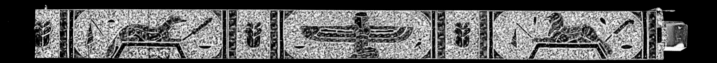

Another Van Cleef & Arpels bracelet of platinum
and diamonds in the same revival style as the one
above. The two dog-like animals and fictional winged
human creature are made of buff-cut sapphires, rubies,
emeralds and onyx. *Collection Van Cleef & Arpels*

A bracelet by Janesich, Paris, c. 1925, featuring the
Sphinx and pyramids; set in platinum with a pavé
diamond background, the images are outlined with
buff-cut diamonds, sapphires, rubies amd onyx.
Private collection. Photo © GIA and Tino Hammid

RIGHT This camel pin in platinum-set pavé diamonds
with a saddle of buff-cut rubies was produced by Van
Cleef & Arpels, c. 1925. *Collection Neil Lane, Los
Angeles. Photo by Tino Hammid*

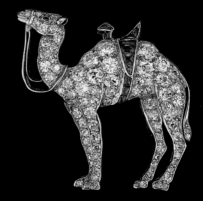

ABOVE This crown in the Egyptian revival style, commissioned from Boucheron by King Fuad I of Egypt in June 1928, depicts a hawk with its wings unfurled. The crown is made of 20K gold, coral, malachite, lapis lazuli and turquoise. *Photo Boucheron Archives*

OPPOSITE An Egyptian revival style pendant of gold and blue enamel in the form of an ibis, 1920s. *Photo courtesy Ulf Breede, Berlin*

Cartier's first tiger brooch from 1928, in platinum and diamonds with onyx stripes. *Collection Art of Cartier. Photo Nick Welch © Cartier*

Sketch for a tiger brooch in diamonds and onyx is from the Mauboussin Archives, 1928.

This brooch of a flying crane in diamonds and platinum accented with a bright-red enamel beak was made by Janesich, Paris, during the 1920s. The illusion of dimension is given to the wings by fancy-cut triangular diamonds and black enamel edging. *Photo Christie's, New York*

A design dated 1930 from the Mauboussin Archives for a brooch depicting a stork in diamonds, rubies and onyx.

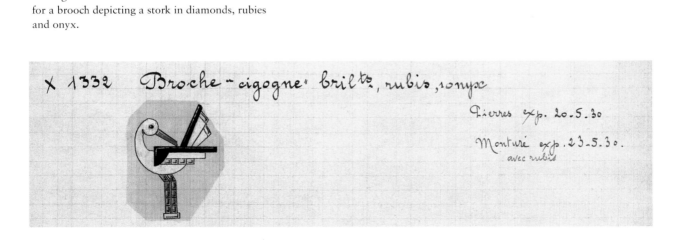

ABOVE This circle clip by Van Cleef & Arpels, 1924, features a bird of buff-cut emeralds, rubies, sapphires and onyx set in platinum and brilliant diamonds. *Photo Van Cleef & Arpels, Paris*

OPPOSITE This wide and highly articulated band bracelet made by Oscar Heyman & Brothers, c. 1925, is decorated with tropical birds on a floral and foliate background, adorned with calibré-cut rubies, sapphires, emeralds and onyx set against brilliant-cut diamonds mounted in platinum. *Photo Sotheby's, Geneva*

BELOW A French articulated platinum and diamond line bracelet from the 1920s bearing a design of four peacocks in buff-cut rubies, sapphires and emeralds. *Photo courtesy Ulf Breede, Berlin*

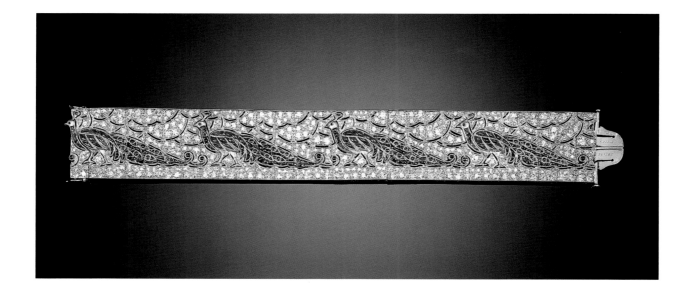

ABOVE Two bird brooches, from 1925 and 1927, made by Van Cleef & Arpels in rose-cut diamonds mounted in platinum. *Collection Van Cleef & Arpels*

OPPOSITE A page from a 1922 Van Cleef & Arpels catalogue, showing a bird clip in diamonds set in platinum. It was fashionable at that time to wear such a clip in a hat with the feathers attached. *Photo Van Cleef & Arpels, Paris*

FOLLOWING PAGES Two cocks fight each other at opposite ends of a jabot brooch by Janesich, Paris, c. 1925. In platinum and diamonds, the menacing birds have tail feathers in calibré-cut emeralds and onyx, while their combs and wattles are in amethysts. *Photo © Historical Design, Inc., New York*

15

ÉPINGLES A CHAPEAUX
& COIFFURES

Dernière Création

HAT AND HAIR PINS

Latest Novelty

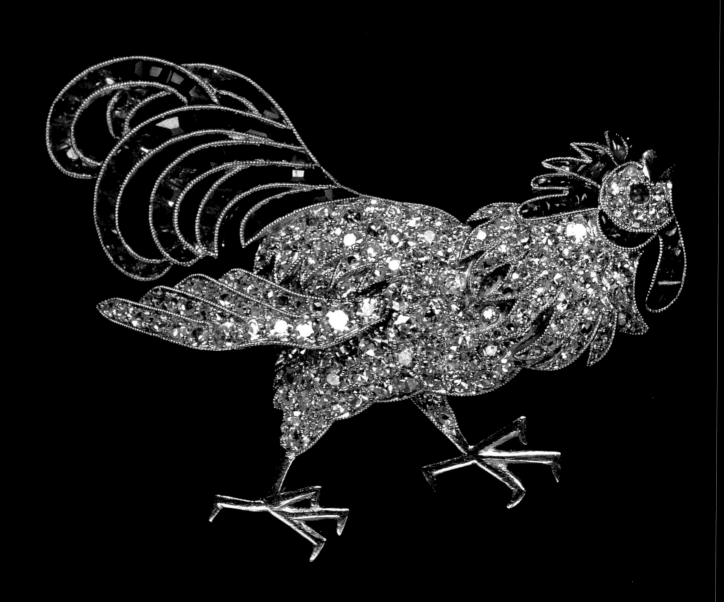

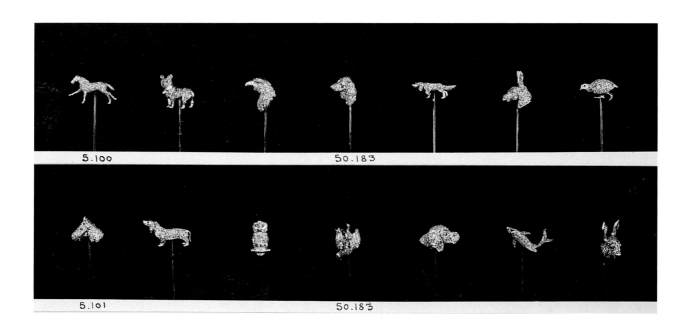

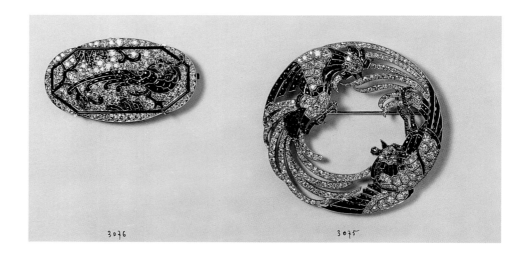

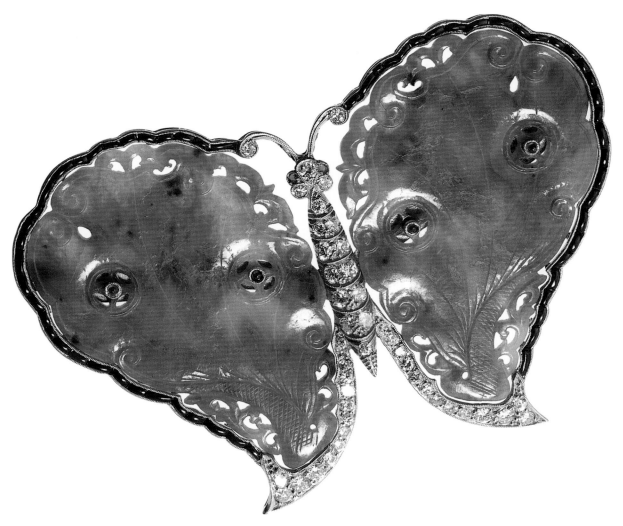

OPPOSITE ABOVE A group of platinum and rose-cut diamond stick pins showing various birds, dogs, horses, donkeys and fish. Atelier Boucheron, November 1921. *Photo Boucheron Archives*

OPPOSITE BELOW Two brooches in platinum, diamonds, emeralds, rubies and sapphires depicting a pheasant in the oval and two fighting cocks in the circle. These were made by Rubel Frères in 1925 for Boucheron. *Photo Boucheron Archives*

ABOVE A French brooch from the late 1920s depicting a butterfly with a body and head of diamonds set in platinum and accented with cabochon ruby eyes. Each wing is carved in green jade, the carving suggesting opposing human faces. The wings are outlined with buff-cut onyx set in platinum. *Photo © Historical Design, Inc., New York*

ABOVE A swallow clip in baguette diamonds and onyx with a pear-shaped diamond head by Van Cleef & Arpels, 1928. *Private collection. Photo Van Cleef & Arpels, Paris*

LEFT A frog pin from the early 1920s in diamonds and onyx mounted in platinum. *Photo courtesy Wartski, London*

Cartier, Paris, made this bracelet in 1929, with two
chimeras in platinum, set with round diamonds and
accented with emeralds and sapphires. *Collection
Art of Cartier. Photo Nick Welch © Cartier*

A jabot pin in the form of a coiled snake. Set
with pavé diamonds and calibré-cut sapphires.
The millegrain edging to the platinum is typical
of the fine work executed in the 1920s.
*Collection HMS Ltd., Beverly Hills, California.
Photo © GIA and Tino Hammid*

A 1920s design from the René Boivin Archives for two
pavé diamond scarab brooches with yellow gold legs
and antennae.

Chapter 4

1930s—'40s
Exuberant Use of Shapes and Gems

The 1930s was a period of transition in the jewelry industry. The stock market crash and the Depression that followed obviously had a devastating effect on business. The jewelry houses that survived, and even flourished, did so because they had the courage to break with tradition and create new styles. Taking a cue from the emerging machine-age aesthetics, their designs rejected the flat rectilinearity of Art Deco and turned to the sculptural and three-dimensional. This style has often been referred to within the jewelry community as "Retro". In fact, however, rather than reflecting the past, it sought to step in tune with developments in the fine and decorative arts, where machine-age concepts and a return to naturalism were occurring simultaneously. The latter was fostered in France and the United States by a few talented designers who used flowers and animals adorning jewelry in exuberant, new designs.

The figure reemerged as a dominant motif, with life restored to subjects. As in previous decades, animal-style jewelry favored images of insects, birds, mammals, sea creatures and reptiles. Color was reintroduced by setting bodies and heads with colored gemstones, and gold replaced platinum as the metal of choice. French houses such as Boucheron, Cartier, Mauboussin, Van Cleef & Arpels and Boivin, and Raymond Yard and Verdura in the United States, excelled in this new style, creating innovative designs, many of which have become icons of their time.

By the third and fourth decades of the twentieth century, a variety of insects, that perennial favorite as a subject for jewelry, were alighting on shoulders and resting on bracelets. Instead of rendering them in precious metals, decorated with diamonds, semi-precious gemstones or enamel, jewelers carved them out of hardstones and invented novel ways to decorate their wings. In 1935, Cartier created a ladybug with a coral body, set with diamonds to form the spots on its back, and black lacquer head and feet. Ten years later, the butterflies they made in yellow gold with coral and black enamel delineating the striations on the wings seemed almost surreal.

It was sheer imagination that inspired the designer at Boucheron who created a piece of jewelry they called "hymenoptera" (the name for the order of four-winged insects which

includes the wasp, the bee and the fly) with ingeniously designed wings. The jeweler used traditional materials for the sapphire-set body, but fabricated the wings out of gold mesh set with diamonds.

Van Cleef & Arpels artfully perched three bees on a bracelet in a honeycomb pattern; each bee detaches and can be worn independently as a brooch. The bracelet functions as both a piece of jewelry and, when not worn, an *objet d'art*. During the 1940s, this venerable firm also transformed its famous ballerina figure into a dragonfly woman, the "*femme libellule*," with her arms extended and wings set with diamonds and sapphires. This image, depicted in the likeness of Tinkerbell from *Peter Pan*, is a modern version of the butterfly woman in Art Nouveau.

In the 1940s there was also a return of birds either portrayed in dynamic stances or captured in endearing poses. The natural beauty of birds could not fail to excite the designer's imagination. Their luxuriant and often iridescent plumage lent itself to brilliant colors in a variety of gemstones. Arguably the most magnificent of them all is the bird of paradise. In this critical period, it became a symbol of the times, with firms such as Cartier, Mauboussin and Van Cleef & Arpels using it as a model in their advertising. Cartier created several sumptuous examples, such as one resting on a perch, with a diamond-set crest and a body divided into gem-set geometric sections ending with long, flowing tail feathers made out of gold links and studded with diamonds. Later in the decade, the firm also offered more modest versions made with plaited gold thread and set with two different colored sapphires.

In 1942, Van Cleef & Arpels created a bold and impressive bird of paradise with swooping wings of calibré-cut rubies and long, trailing tail feathers of calibré-cut sapphires. This and Cartier's flamingo brooch, designed by Jeanne Toussaint for the Duchess of Windsor in 1940, are perhaps the two most celebrated bird ornaments in the history of jewelry design.

Both Cartier and Van Cleef & Arpels designed more wearable birds than their ambitious birds of paradise. Some of the most famous are those locked in cages, designed for Cartier by Jeanne Toussaint and Peter Lemarchand to protest the occupation of France during World War II. When the war was finally over, the bird flew out of its cage, singing a song of joy. The house of Boivin also designed a series of metaphorical birds: patriotic eagles announcing the French resistance at the outbreak of war and, when peace was declared, a rooster symbolizing the French fighting spirit.

Most of the bird jewels created during this period were wearable pieces, some designed in unusual settings, such as Van Cleef & Arpels's birds nestled into straw hats; others advancing modernistic concepts, such as Maurice Duvalet's 1941 abstract bird whose citrine body looks more like a creature from a Miró painting than a piece of jewelry. At Boivin, Madame Germaine Boivin introduced the first birds into their repertoire with a pavé-set diamond bird embellished with engraved rubies and emerald beads. In 1939, with the war raging at their back door, Juliette Moutard created a dove, the symbol of peace, carrying a pavé diamond heart wrapped in an emerald garland.

OPPOSITE This charming pair of ladybug ear clips was made by Cartier, Paris, 1936, and belonged to the singer Marian Anderson. The bodies are made of coral with diamond collet spots, while the head and legs are black lacquer; mounted in white gold. *Collection Art of Cartier*

ABOVE A dragonfly brooch with a woman's body (known as "Wings of Victory"), designed by John Rubel for Van Cleef & Arpels, New York, 1949. *Photo Van Cleef & Arpels, Paris*

BELOW A design by Juliette Moutard, 1939, from the René Boivin Archives for a brooch depicting a gold and sapphire dove carrying a heart of pavé diamonds wrapped in an emerald garland. As a universal symbol of peace, the dove reflected the concerns of the troubled era in which the jewel was designed.

ABOVE A design from the Tiffany & Co. Archives, c. 1930, for a swordfish pin of buff-cut sapphires and pavé diamonds.

BELOW This turtle brooch from the 1940s by Seaman Schepps has a shell composed of large faceted sapphires prong-set in gold. The head and legs are pavé diamonds set in platinum, and cabochon rubies serve as the eyes. *Photo Seaman Schepps, New York*

BOTTOM Two 1940s dachshund brooches by Cartier made of buff-topped citrines set in gold. *Photos © Historical Design, Inc., New York; and Courtesy Sandra Cronan, Ltd., London*

OPPOSITE A selection of jeweled cats by Cartier, Paris, that were prominent in the collection of the Duchess of Windsor. Designed by Jeanne Toussaint in the 1950s, the tigers are pavé-set fancy yellow diamonds with onyx stripes set in yellow gold, while the panthers are pavé colorless diamonds with onyx spots set in platinum. The panther perched on the cabochon sapphire ball was the first cat made for the Duchess in 1949, and it has squarish and triangular-cut sapphire spots set on a pavé diamond body. *Photo Sotheby's, Geneva*

Perhaps the best-known piece of animal jewelry from this period is the Cartier panther, a diamond and sapphire cat sitting on top of a 152.35-carat cabochon sapphire. Commissioned in 1949 by the Duke and Duchess of Windsor and nicknamed 'The Panther', it too was conceived by Jeanne Toussaint in collaboration with Peter Lemarchand. Their continued association resulted in the creation of Cartier's "great cat menagerie".

During World War II, colored gemstones such as amethysts, tourmalines and citrines became an integral part of jewelry design. Cartier created an amusing dachshund with sherry colored buff-cut citrines cut into appropriate shapes to form the body, head and legs. In the United States, a few designers working outside the larger concerns made imaginative animal designs. After opening his own salon in New York in 1939, Fulco Santostefano delle Cerda, duc di Verdura began to produce fanciful jewels, with an eye for design and color, that were not reliant upon expensive gemstones. He would, for example, incorporate an ivory camel chess piece into a brooch, adorned with a rider and appropriate riding accoutrements. Raymond Yard, who catered to an elite clientele, designed a series of brooches of rabbit and chicken waiters, each standing erect and fully dressed down to the bow tie, all in precious gemstones.

Sea creatures were treated with special attention at the house of Boivin. Beginning in the 1920s they created a selection of brooches, earrings and necklaces with different shells. In 1935, Juliette Moutard designed the original starfish brooch for the actress Claudette Colbert. Her conception was unlike anything that had ever been created before: each arm was articulated, its motion simulating the actual movement of the starfish on the ocean floor. This basic design, executed in various sizes and gemstones, remained in production for many years.

The slow and steady turtle appears to be floating on a brooch by Seaman Schepps, who popularized gem-studded jewelry in which the animal is captured in some sort of activity. The turtle, with its head slightly cocked and its legs in repose at the side of its body, appears to be leisurely drifting in water. Sapphires make up the segmented shell.

Boivin also created a unique member of the reptile family, a chameleon that, like the natural specimen, changes the color of its skin. At the press of the lizard's tongue, its flanks rotate, one side red and the other green, or a variation of both. Other than the chameleon and a few snakes designed by this firm as well as by Boucheron, reptiles seemed to have been a neglected member of the bestiary during the 1930s and '40s. By this period, there was less emphasis on symbolic meaning assigned to jewels and more on their aesthetic appeal. For this reason, birds, butterflies and other alluring creatures were far more in demand.

ABOVE A pair of butterfly earrings from Cartier, Paris, 1943, with baguette diamond bodies, triangular diamond heads, and coral wings studded with bezel-set cabochon emeralds. *Photo Christie's, Geneva*

OPPOSITE These two butterfly brooches were made by Cartier, Paris, in 1945, and belonged to the actress Josette Day. They are set in yellow gold with wings of coral and black and white enamel, accented with cabochon emeralds. The bodies are coral and the antennae terminate with diamonds. *Collection Art of Cartier. Photo Nick Welch © Cartier*

MAUBOUSSIN.

l'Officiel de la Couture Juin 1941

ABOVE An advertisement in *L'Officiel de la Couture*, July 1941, featuring designs by Mauboussin for butterfly brooches. *Mauboussin Archives*

OPPOSITE A 1940s pin from Van Cleef & Arpels that is a variation of the popular *"fille libellule"* or girl with dragonfly wings, with a rose-cut diamond head, a ruby head ornament and faceted sapphire wings. *Photo courtesy Nelson Rarities, Inc., Portland, Maine*

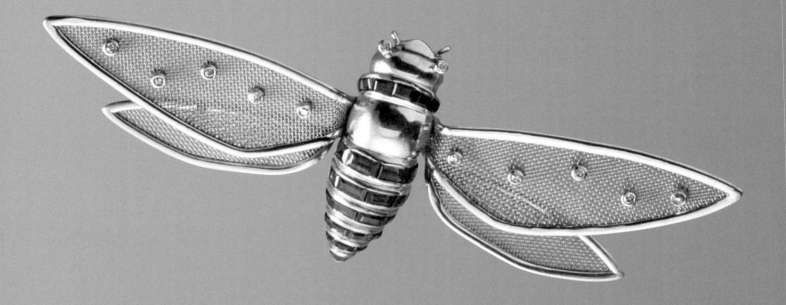

ABOVE This "hymenoptera" clip by Boucheron, 1944, spreads wings of gold mesh, sprinkled with bezel-set diamonds. The body is polished gold set with calibré-cut sapphires. *Collection Boucheron*

OPPOSITE A brooch in the shape of a camel chess piece designed by Fulco di Verdura in the 1940s. Made of ivory, the camel carries a saddle of colored stones with a gold, enamel and diamond rider. *Photo Verdura, New York*

BELOW A honeycomb "Ludo" bracelet decorated with detachable bee clips by Van Cleef & Arpels, 1947. Fabricated in 18K yellow gold, the bees have bodies of cabochon rubies and ceylon sapphires with wings and heads set with diamonds. *Private collection. Photo Van Cleef & Arpels, Paris*

OPPOSITE This elaborate bird of paradise brooch by Van Cleef & Arpels, Paris, 1942, has a body of polished and engraved gold with feathers of calibré-cut rubies and sapphires. The head has a cabochon ruby eye and a beak of pavé diamonds set in platinum. *Photo Van Cleef & Arpels, Paris*

ABOVE RIGHT A stylized bird clip with a citrine body, rose-cut diamond head and polished gold wings and tail, designed by Maurice Duvalet for Van Cleef & Arpels, New York in 1940. *Private collection. Photo Van Cleef & Arpels, Paris*

ABOVE Another design of Maurice Duvalet for Van Cleef & Arpels, New York, dated 1949. In this whimsical brooch a platinum and diamond bird is perched in a hat of woven gold with ruby, sapphire and diamond flowers in the "Hawaii" style. *Photo Van Cleef & Arpels, Paris*

RIGHT This 1940s swan brooch by Seaman Schepps, in platinum and diamonds, has a large baroque pearl as its body and a small cabochon emerald as the eye. *Photo Seaman Schepps, New York*

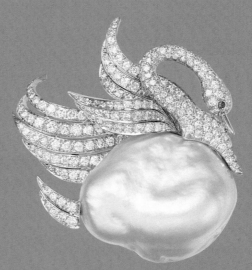

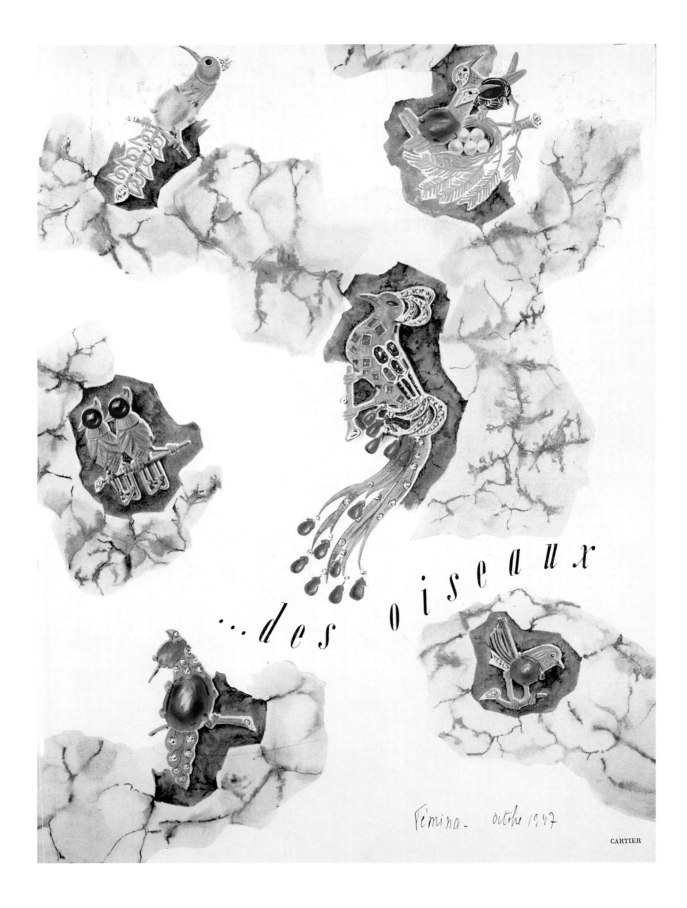

...des oiseaux

Fémina— octobre 1947

CARTIER

OPPOSITE A Cartier advertisement of bird brooches published in *Femina,* October 1947. *Collection Art of Cartier. Photo Nick Welch © Cartier*

ABOVE A peacock with an articulated tail holds tightly to a branch in this brooch by Cartier, Paris, c. 1947. The jewel is made of engraved gold set with sapphires, emeralds and diamonds with ruby drops suspended from the tail feathers. *Private collection. Photo © GIA and Tino Hammid*

Two diamond snakes wind around an onyx background on this gold and silver bangle made by Boucheron, c. 1935. The edges are trimmed with diamonds and calibré-cut coral. *Collection Boucheron*

This chameleon brooch was an innovative creation from René Boivin, 1939. It is composed of yellow gold, rubies and emeralds, with eyes of tiger's eye. Depressing the tongue causes the body to rotate, thereby changing color, as does a chameleon. *Photo René Boivin*

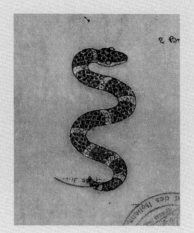

ABOVE Designs of the 1930s and '40s for serpent jewelry from the René Boivin Archives. The two coiled serpents are designs from 1948. The S-shaped serpent brooch in yellow gold and enamel is an early design from 1935. The yellow gold snake suspending a yellow stone from its mouth is an earring with the tail coiling up the ear.

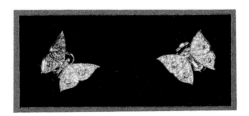

TOP A platinum and diamond charm bracelet, made by Pierre Sterlé for Boucheron in July 1938, featuring a monkey, a pig, lovebirds, a turtle, a dog and a rocking horse. *Photo Boucheron Archives*

ABOVE A pair of butterfly earclips in platinum and diamonds, March 1938. *Photo Boucheron Archives*

RIGHT Three platinum-set pavé diamond and baguette butterflies that can be worn as clips in the hair or on clothing, 1937. *Photo Boucheron Archives*

OPPOSITE A group of whimsical brooches in polished gold featuring animals performing human activities, made by David for Boucheron, November 1948. *Photo Boucheron Archives*

Two 1930s platinum and pavé diamond pins from
Raymond Yard, depicting a rooster courting a chicken
decked out as a lady. The rooster is flashing his tricolor
enamel tail while delivering two ruby cosmopolitans on
an enamel tray. The chicken, wearing an enamel and
pavé diamond hat and a diamond necklace, is shaded
by a green enamel and diamond parasol.
Photo Raymond Yard, New York

Three whimsical rabbit pins made by Raymond Yard
during the 1930s. In platinum-set pavé diamonds, the
rabbits, dressed as waiters, are wearing tails accented
by calibré-cut emeralds, rubies and sapphires. The
shoes, ties and trays are gold and enamel.
Photo Raymond Yard, New York

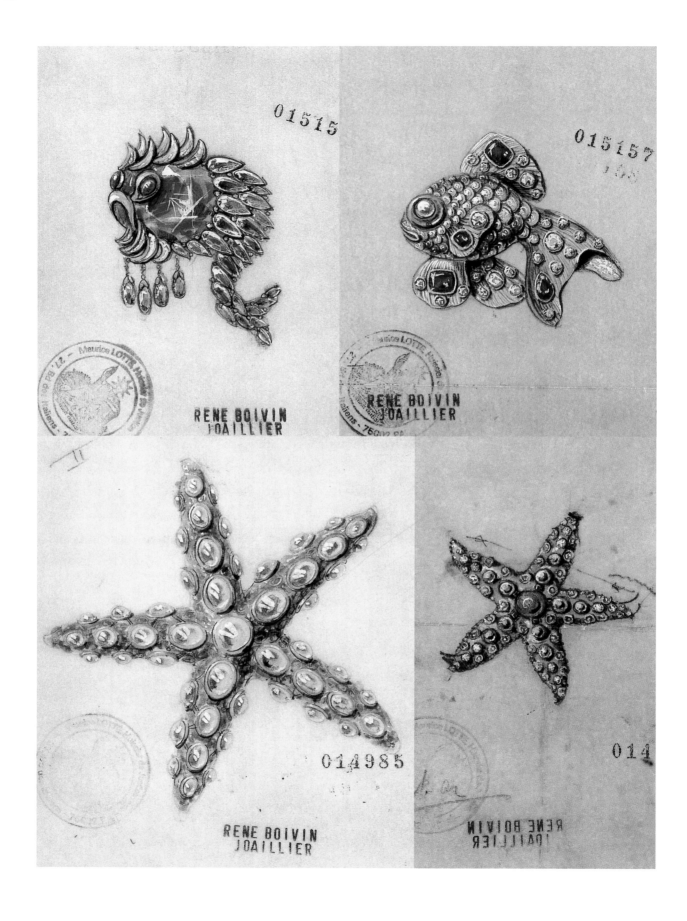

RENE BOIVIN
IOAILLIER

OPPOSITE ABOVE From the René Boivin Archives, a 1949 design for a tropical fish clip with gold and diamond scales and decorated with emerald markings; and a 1950 design for a fish clip in aquamarine with ruby eyes. The scales are represented by pear-shaped aquamarines, while the gills are polished gold set with diamonds.

OPPOSITE BELOW From the René Boivin Archives, two designs for starfish brooches: one from 1938 featured large moonstones set in gold with faceted aquamarines as the background; the other, from 1940, was to be executed in pearls and emeralds set in yellow gold.

ABOVE A 1949 design for a clip in the form of a fish featuring a large faceted aquamarine head, a rose-cut diamond eye and scales made of cabochon sapphires set in gold. *René Boivin Archives*

011034

RENE BOIVIN
JOAILLIER

From the René Boivin Archives, two designs dated
January 1939 by Germaine Boivin of bulls' skulls
adorned with jeweled flowers and ribbons.

0110

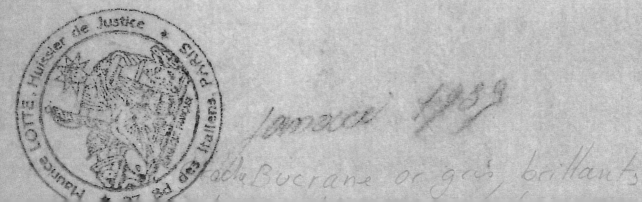

Chapter 5

1950s—'60s
Dynamic, Adventurous Designs

This period was one of affluence, when a large segment of the population enjoyed the benefits of wealth. Fine jewelry was no longer just a province of the rich; the middle class could now afford precious stone jewelry and were eager to emulate the trendsetters of the day. Two of these became true icons in the world of fashion: Grace Kelly, the popular actress whose marriage to Prince Rainier III of Monaco captivated the world; and Jacqueline Kennedy, a quiet socialite of elegant and urbane manner who was catapulted into international prominence when her husband, Senator John Fitzgerald Kennedy, was elected President of the United States in 1960. The social environment had gradually changed, with formal entertaining giving way to cocktail parties where everyone wanted to dress in the latest fashions. Glamour was 'in', amply supported by a broad range of jewelry styles, from sumptuous diamond creations to colorful, artfully designed creatures from the animal kingdom that could be either serious or simply fun.

The variety and quantity of animal-style jewelry from the 1950s and '60s parallels in many respects the fascination for the same subject in the Victorian period. At both times, animals abounded on all types of jewelry, from simple everyday pieces to diamond-studded splendors worn only for special occasions. Practically all jewelry houses and designers focused their attention on making animals in a variety of poses for every type of jewelry imaginable. Adopting images from climates ranging from the tropics to Antarctica, they rendered them realistically, appealing like pets or, with a bit of artistic license, in whimsical forms and expressions. Whatever their representations, animals were everywhere!

As in the Victorian period, butterflies fluttered their way into just about every jewelry house. Most often, the wings on this perennial favorite were set with diamonds or colored gemstones. Jean Schlumberger, who worked in Paris before coming to New York and joining Tiffany & Co. in 1956, was always looking for the unique in the mundane. His masterful designs pulsate with life. On one pair of bracelets he set six butterflies at oblique angles, every one of them different in shape and size, and set with different gemstones accenting their diamond or gold bodies. When this tour de force of design is worn, the gold antennae and pointed decorative motifs on the wings jut out at unpredictable angles, with a high probability of snagging the fabric of the wearer's dress. In Paris, Mauboussin created a butterfly brooch using techniques not seen since the turn of the century. Instead of covering the wings with precious gem material, they used cloisonné enamel in green, blue and gold tones, setting the 'eyes' with cabochon rubies and emeralds. This imaginative use of materials extends to the insect's body, with carved emeralds forming the segments of the upper section, rows of diamonds forming the lower part.

Bees and beetles flew and crawled on shoulders in inventively designed brooches, often incorporating coral and onyx into the design, a combination of gemstones previously employed in Art Deco jewelry for its stark color contrast. By the 1960s, these gemstones demarcated entire segments of the insect's anatomy. The house of Hermès, best known for beautiful scarves, created a pair of stag beetles with coral bodies and onyx heads. Fulco di Verdura transformed the omnipresent bee that had been a source of inspiration for over a hundred years into a gem-set creation with a coral body, onyx head and wings formed out of enormous pear-shaped diamonds.

The creature most representative of animal jewelry in the 1950s and '60s is clearly the bird. Nature offers a seemingly infinite variety of these endearing creatures whose bodies and wings provide a canvas upon which designers can express their creativity. During this period, jewelry designers took full advantage of this opportunity, either injecting new ideas on previous designs or carving out new niches from revolutionary design concepts. The luscious bird of paradise lent itself to outstanding examples of the former as it was portrayed actively swooping onto a branch or, having just landed, sitting there demurely. Mauboussin illustrated five such examples in *Connaissance des Arts* in 1958, each bird set with carved rubies, emeralds or sapphires to provide texture and three-dimensionality.

Fulco di Verdura's bird designs have a pictorial quality. He created swans, falcons, owls and the long extinct dodo with baroque pearl bodies, reminiscent of jewels from the Renaissance, that soften the all-white look of diamond-set platinum heads, tail feathers and wings.

On other pieces, a mother bird, made out of platinum and diamonds, shelters her eight cabochon sapphire eggs with her wings. Verdura's jewels are not only beautifully designed but also fun, fun to wear and fun just to look at.

Perhaps the most noted designer of birds in this period is Pierre Sterlé. His bird brooches surpass anything that had been done before, establishing a distinctive style that no one has since duplicated. Woodpeckers, seagulls, pheasants, owls, cockatoos, herons, partridges, toucans, parrots are designed and crafted in exquisite detail, and convey a sense of life and movement. Heads and bodies may be diamond-set or modeled out of a faceted colored gemstone, while wings and tail feathers are formed out of several engraved gold

ABOVE Two early 1950s designs from the René Boivin Archives for brooches depicting squirrels. In citrines or topazes, the squirrels sport calibré-cut sapphire or cabochon ruby stripes down their backs.

OPPOSITE This imaginative butterfly pin was created by Verdura, c. 1960. It has a coral body and four large pear-shaped diamonds as the wings; its head is an onyx ball. *Photo Verdura, New York*

BELOW A Verdura design of the 1950s for a dodo with a body formed by a large baroque pearl, a beak of coral, and neck and tail feathers of pavé diamonds. *Verdura Archives*

This elephant clip by Jean Schlumberger, 1967, has a gray transparent enamel head, ruby eyes and a trunk in *ciselé* gold adorned with square-cut emeralds. The tusks are made of white onyx and the ears are pavé diamonds set in platinum. The animal is decorated with a headpiece of gray and gold spinels set in a lattice motif and a fringe of pear-shaped turquoise drops. *Photo Tiffany & Co.*

A bracelet by David Webb, New York, c. 1965, of a lioness's head in 18K gold and diamonds with emerald eyes and decorated with a cabochon ruby on the head. *Photo courtesy Primavera Gallery, New York*

feathers or gold loop-in-loop chains that flutter when the brooch is worn. Most are 3 to 4 inches in length and, when worn in multiples, have a great impact.

Whimsy is also a characteristic of other birds from this period. Boivin, for example, created a clip in the guise of a hen but showing only its head protruding above two tiers of feathers turned upwards at the tips. It is inventive in its construction, giving the impression of a finger puppet. Almost as popular as birds, warm-blooded mammals were well represented in animal jewelry of this period, portrayed in a wide range of images as pets, ferocious beasts or dressed in suits, imitating humans. At Tiffany's, two designers were personalizing their styles. Jean Schlumberger bedecked an elephant head with an elaborate gold headdress, complete with dangling turquoise. Donald Claflin turned to fanciful animals based on story book characters and imaginary creatures such as the walrus from "The Walrus and the Carpenter" or a fully dressed hippopotamus.

David Webb is a well-known name in the world of animal-style jewelry from the 1960s. He reintroduced bangles with animal head terminals, similar in overall design to ancient examples or to those in the archeological style of the nineteenth century. However, instead of adopting the earlier structure of two semicircular gold sections hinged at the middle with animal heads at the terminals, Webb's bracelets are fully articulated for ease of movement, enameled in a variety of colors and lavishly set with diamonds and other precious gemstones. He executed this design for an assortment of animals, including horses, zebras, elephants, fish, bulls, rams, frogs and lions, which were never categorized in a particular series but referred to simply as "Animal Jewelry".

By the 1960s, immortalizing one's pet into a jewelry form had become popular. Several jewelers went along with this vogue, including Van Cleef & Arpels with its poodle brooches, Boivin with a variety of dog images (such as dachshunds and golden retrievers), and Verdura with cocker spaniels, poodles and playful cats. Big, ferocious cats also abounded on jewelry. Cartier continued its "Great Cat" series with panthers calmly sitting on branches and, for Barbara Hutton, tigers with yellow diamonds and onyx stripes on a bracelet, brooch and earrings, the latter two designed in the style of the Golden Fleece. Verdura crowned his jungle cats, while Boivin crafted lions either in a reclining pose or imitating a throw rug made with the stretched out animal skin.

Sea life in jewelry took on a different character from that in the previous decades. Now it was lavishly gem-set with unusual materials or shaped into interesting forms. Cartier made an atypical fish out of watermelon tourmaline, and Van Cleef & Arpels created three blowfish, each with a huge cabochon sapphire body. For Schlumberger, circular-cut diamonds set into cloisonné-style mountings served as suitable alternatives to represent scales on his dolphin clip. Seaman Schepps floated a fish atop a baroque pearl sea wall or placed a pearl between the claws of a gem-encrusted crab. Boivin continued the theme of movable parts by dangling stones from the arms of a starfish or making the creature three-dimensional with cabochon stones for the suckers. Probably the most imaginative starfish designed in this period is thought to have been created by Salvador Dalí in the 1960s. The flexible construction of this brooch enables the arms of the starfish to twist, turn and fall in a way similar to those of the real sea creature. Two butterfly enhancements can be fitted over the arms and, with an attachment, the brooch turns into a hand ornament.

Imaginative jewels were also the purview of the reptilian world, especially at Cartier's where clients commissioned special pieces. For the French actress, Jacqueline Delubac, Jeanne Toussaint created a special lizard clip brooch set with graduated diamonds along its back. Although reminiscent of similar pieces of the nineteenth century, this lizard differs in several respects: texturing along the body imitates the lizard's skin, the tail is articulated and the head is movable. The static pose of the 1880s was transformed into an active version of the real creature. Another Cartier designer, Gabriel Raton, working under the direction of Toussaint, readapted the snake motif from the previous century into a magnificent creation, featuring 2,473 diamonds on the top side and a multi-colored enamel design on the underside. Commissioned by the Mexican film actress, Maria Felix, this piece can be worn with either side showing.

Unicorns, dragons and chimeras continued to be the most popular images in the world of fantasy. The beloved medieval representation of the unicorn is adapted into sweet renditions with heads that resemble horses outfitted with twisted horns. Verdura created a fiery dragon with its red tongue protruding, while Donald Claflin's dragon smiles at us. Chimeras could be set within a pendant, as in one made at Boivin, or become the focal point on bracelets as on Cartier's bangles. Although this theme signifies a recurrence of Cartier's repertoire from the late 1920s, the new bracelets are designed in a modern format, carved out of coral and accented with diamonds along the bangle as well as to delineate the mouth, eyes and hair of the creature. Other variations on this theme included a bracelet with rows of ribbed beads and a chimera's head clip set with diamonds.

The two decades after World War II were a time when fashion-conscious women sought a great variety of animal-style jewelry, designed with either precious or colored gemstones not only for color but to add another dimension. Fortunately, new jewelers emerged to meet this demand and the established fraternity were quick to adapt their styles to the new look.

A double fish brooch in pavé diamonds with red enamel fins and tails, designed by Jean Schlumberger for Tiffany & Co., 1965. *Photo © Tiffany & Co.*

ABOVE A 1960s design from the René Boivin Archives for a starfish brooch in gold, emeralds and faceted amethysts. (This design has has six points instead of the usual five.)

LEFT The fox in this gold clip by Boucheron, 1967, has ruby eyes and is dressed for a special occasion in a blue, green and red enamel suit. *Collection Boucheron*

OPPOSITE A large butterfly clip by Mauboussin, c. 1965, in yellow gold, translucent cloisonné enamel, diamonds, calibré-cut sapphires, cabochon rubies and carved emeralds. *Photo Mauboussin, Paris*

ABOVE Two 1960s designs from the Mauboussin Archives for butterfly brooches in gold with translucent cloisonné enamel and multicolored stones.

The handwritten labels on the designs read:

Papillon brillants saphirs

Papillon brillants, turquoises, rubis, émeraudes

Clips papillons, brillants, saphirs, rubis, émeraudes

ABOVE Two 1950s designs for butterfly clips in diamonds, sapphires, rubies and emeralds by René-Sim Lacaze to be produced by Mauboussin. *Mauboussin Archives*

LEFT A pair of stag beetle scatter pins in 18K gold, coral and onyx by Hermès, Paris, c. 1965. *Photo courtesy Primavera Gallery, New York*

A group of 1960s designs from the Mauboussin
Archives for bee pins in gold, diamonds and onyx; and
various insect pins in gold, diamonds, coral and onyx.

This pin by Marchak, Paris, 1960s, has a pink tourmaline and diamond butterfly perched on a flower of peridots. *Photo courtesy Primavera Gallery, New York*

These two fabulous butterfly bracelets by Jean Schlumberger, 1956, for Tiffany & Co., combine to make a dog collar necklace. They are executed in amethysts, sapphires, peridots, turquoises, spinels, platinum-set colorless diamonds, and gold-set pavé yellow diamonds. *Photo © Tiffany & Co.*

011136

ABOVE This unusual design for a butterfly brooch from the René Boivin Archives, 1950, calls for large rectangular-cut sapphires on the wings.

RIGHT A 1950s design from the Seaman Schepps Archives for a butterfly brooch in gold, diamonds and multicolored cabochon or carved stones.

Birds designed by Pierre Sterlé, Paris, c. 1960:

LEFT A tropical bird perched on a textured gold branch, with faceted labradorite body, citrine face, platinum and pavé diamond beak and plumage, and textured gold tail feathers. Below it is a swooping kingfisher with a polished labradorite head and body, textured gold plumage, pavé diamond eyes, and beak and feather accents. *Photo © GIA and Tino Hammid*

OPPOSITE Four birds, including a toucan and one imaginatively stylized, combining platinum, pavé diamonds, gold fringe, tourmalines, a baroque pearl, coral, and other gemstones in various combinations. *Photo © GIA and Tino Hammid*

FOLLOWING PAGES More birds by Pierre Sterlé. *From left to right*, a bird of paradise with rubellite body, fringed gold crest, mother-of-pearl tail feathers and pavé diamond and platinum beak, head and tail accents; a swallow-tailed bird with rubellite body, pearl head, and gold-fringed plumage; a bee-eater with faceted citrine body and stylized plumage of textured gold and pavé diamonds in platinum; a parrot with a beaded gold head, green sapphire body with textured gold tail feathers and pavé diamond and platinum accents, winking a diamond eye over its shoulder; and an exotic bird fluffing its feathers on an emerald-set gold branch, with an emerald-cut diamond eye and plumage of textured gold and pavé diamonds in platinum. *Photos © GIA and Tino Hammid*

This 1960s Verdura brooch is in the shape of a platinum and diamond swan with a baroque pearl body and a coral beak. Below it is a drawing from the archives for another platinum and diamond swan brooch sporting an emerald necklace. *Photos Verdura, New York*

ABOVE A 1966 brooch by Verdura of a hen in diamonds
and platinum. With an onyx beak, coral crest, cabochon
ruby eyes and gold-tipped feathers, it is nesting eight
large cabochon sapphire eggs. *Photo Verdura, New York*

RIGHT A duck's head brooch made by Cartier, Paris,
1953, and formerly in the Duchess of Windsor's
collection. It is constructed from a baroque pearl, inset
with bezel-set emeralds, a sapphire eye and a coral beak.
Collection Art of Cartier. Photo Nick Welch © Cartier

ABOVE Bird brooches, c. 1960. (*Left*) Exotic bird typical of the designs of Marchak, Paris, perched on a branch, with a ruby crest, diamond neck feathers, marquise-cut emerald body and gold-fringed tail tipped with diamonds. (*Centre*) A stylized bird of paradise by Mauboussin, perched on a gold branch with a carved emerald body, tail feathers in carved rubies and engraved gold, a faceted ruby eye and calibré sapphire crest feathers.

(*Right*) A Mauboussin parrot with a carved emerald and ruby body, pavé diamond wing tips and turquoise and sapphire cabochon head and tail. *Private collection. Photo © GIA and Tino Hammid*

OPPOSITE Two of the brooches from this page (centre and right) appear in a Mauboussin advertisement featuring bird brooches from 1958–60.

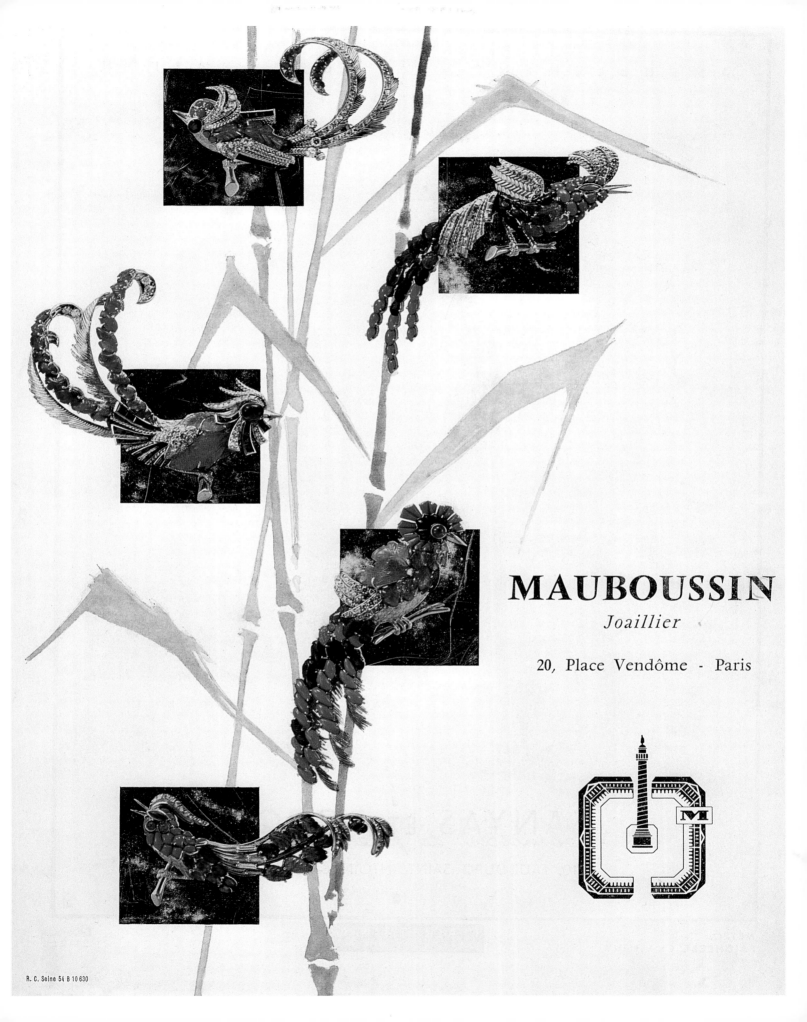

MAUBOUSSIN

Joaillier

20, Place Vendôme - Paris

R. C. Seine 54 B 10 630

OPPOSITE This owl brooch by Cartier, Paris, 1954, has an 18K yellow gold body set with yellow diamonds. The wings are faceted sapphires, and the faceted sapphire eyes are circled by rings of colorless diamonds. *Collection Art of Cartier. Photo Nick Welch © Cartier*

RIGHT A gold and platinum humming-bird brooch by Van Cleef & Arpels, 1963. The bird, sitting on a diamond and gold branch, has a ruby eye, sapphire head, and marquise-shaped emerald body with pavé diamond feathers and accents. *Private collection. Photo Van Cleef & Arpels, Paris*

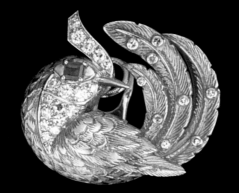

ABOVE These two humming-bird brooches were designed by Verdura in gold, platinum, diamonds and enamel, 1960s. *Private collection. Photo courtesy Neil Lane, Los Angeles*

BELOW A pair of lovebird earrings made by Cartier, London, 1960. They are in gold and pavé diamonds with ruby eyes as accents. *Private collection. Photo © GIA and Tino Hammid*

ABOVE A whimsical rooster dress clip made by René Boivin, 1950, in heavy chased gold with emeralds and sapphires set on its feathers and comb and wattle set with rubies.

RIGHT AND BELOW A similar Boivin rooster headdress clip, 1951, has a circular ruff of gold feathers set with yellow diamonds, while the comb is set with emeralds. The matching pair of earrings has the stylized feather motif around pear-shaped emeralds. *Photos © GIA and Tino Hammid, courtesy Fred Leighton*

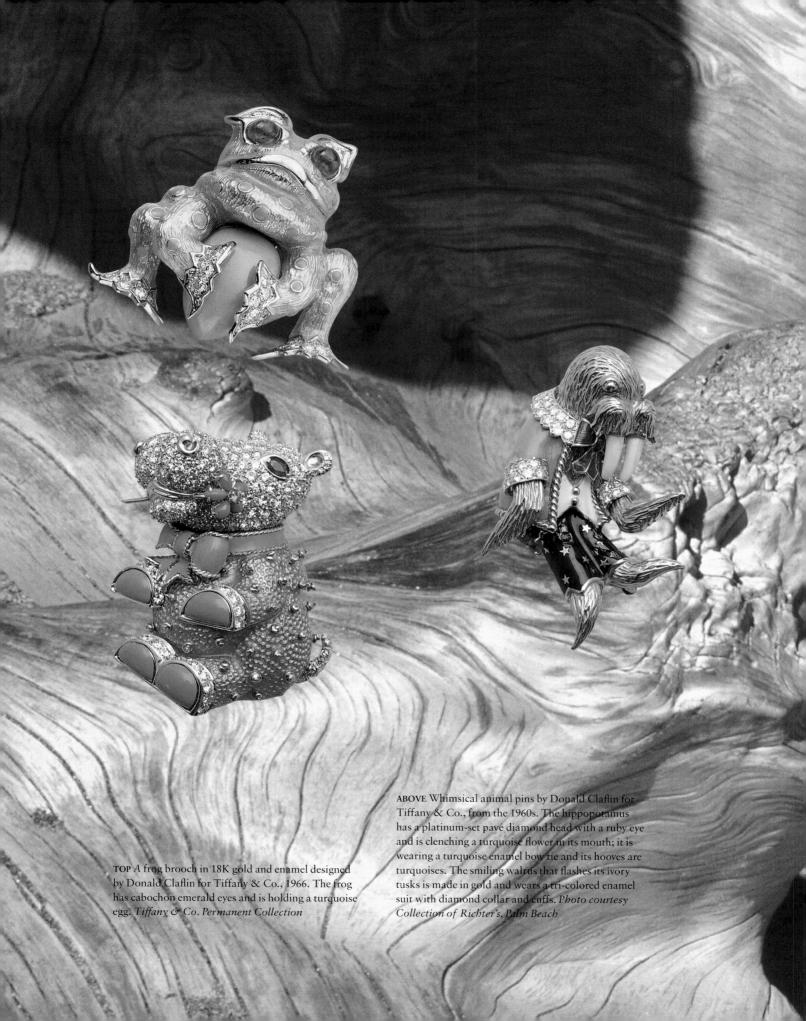

TOP A frog brooch in 18K gold and enamel designed by Donald Claflin for Tiffany & Co., 1966. The frog has cabochon emerald eyes and is holding a turquoise egg. *Tiffany & Co. Permanent Collection*

ABOVE Whimsical animal pins by Donald Claflin for Tiffany & Co., from the 1960s. The hippopotamus has a platinum-set pavé diamond head with a ruby eye and is clenching a turquoise flower in its mouth; it is wearing a turquoise enamel bow tie and its hooves are turquoises. The smiling walrus that flashes its ivory tusks is made in gold and wears a tri-colored enamel suit with diamond collar and cuffs. *Photo courtesy Collection of Richter's, Palm Beach*

RIGHT By Donald Claflin for Tiffany & Co., c. 1960, this dragon pin is primarily pavé diamonds set in platinum with gold scales down its back, cabochon ruby eyes, a pear-shaped ruby mouth and gold claws. *Photo courtesy Collection of Richter's, Palm Beach*

BELOW A brooch in the shape of a winged dragon, designed by Claflin for Tiffany & Co., 1960. In gold and platinum-set pavé diamonds, its body encircles a spherical turquoise, while the head sparkles with emerald eyes and a suspended pear-shaped ruby hangs from its mouth. *Tiffany & Co. Permanent Collection*

ABOVE Six poodle charms adorn this 18K gold hollow large curb link bracelet. Charm bracelets of this type were particularly popular in the 1950s and '60s. *Private collection. Photo © GIA and Tino Hammid*

OPPOSITE The angelic poodle in this pendant brooch by William Ruser of Beverly Hills, 1950s, sits up and begs in a cloud of freshwater pearls, while its earring friends wait their turn. Each 14K gold poodle has a freshwater pearl halo and wings as well as sapphire eyes. *Private collection. Photo © GIA and Tino Hammid*

ABOVE A poodle brooch by Verdura, 1950s, in platinum and diamonds with a ruby eye. *Private collection. Photo Verdura, New York*

LEFT A French poodle pin by Van Cleef & Arpels, New York, 1952, in diamonds and 18K gold. The pampered pet wears a ruby collar. *Private collection. Photo © GIA and Tino Hammid*

BELOW Two designs from the René Boivin Archives for brooches depicting dogs. The Labrador retriever is dated 1950, the dachshunds 1965.

OPPOSITE ABOVE This clip portraying a dog's head, by Cartier, Paris, from the 1960s, is made of engraved 18K gold, with ears of flexible mesh, accented by diamonds set in platinum. The eyes are marquise-shaped rubies and the nose is onyx. *Private collection. Photo © GIA and Tino Hammid*

OPPOSITE BELOW A pair of gold, yellow diamond and diamond earrings in the form of stylized cats' heads, by an unidentified designer, c. 1960. *Photo by David Behl, courtesy Camilla Dietz Bergeron, Ltd., New York*

OPPOSITE An early 1960s panther brooch by Cartier, Paris, made of platinum with pavé diamonds, onyx spots and pear-shaped emerald eyes. The cat is comfortably stretched out on a coral branch. *Photo courtesy Firestone and Parson, Boston*

ABOVE LEFT A dress clip by Cartier, Paris, 1967, of a gold, yellow diamond and onyx tiger with pear-shaped emerald eyes peering out of lapis lazuli foliage. *Private collection. Photo by Harold and Erica Van Pelt © GIA*

ABOVE RIGHT Verdura's late 1950s version of the panther brooch has the animal wearing a gold crown with diamonds and rubies and an emerald necklace with a pearl drop. *Verdura Archives*

OPPOSITE AND ABOVE This yellow gold, yellow diamond and onyx tiger clip with articulated legs and tail belonged to Barbara Hutton and was made by Cartier, Paris, 1957. Hutton specially ordered the pair of matching earrings from Cartier in 1961. *Collection Art of Cartier. Photos Nick Welch © Cartier*

ABOVE RIGHT A 1960 design from the René Boivin Archives shows a gold and diamond leopard brooch. The spots are represented by cabochon sapphires while the eyes are marquise-shaped emeralds.

1091 E 888.

1093 E 890

1094 E 891.

1095 E 892.

842 99 12

1096

E 895

1096 + 1097

893 E 894

OPPOSITE ABOVE A bracelet of alternating cabochon ruby and sapphire diagonal stripes separated by diamond lines, made by Bulgari, c. 1960. The two lions' masks with thick pavé diamond manes guard a large cabochon sapphire between their mouths. *Photo Bulgari, New York*

OPPOSITE BELOW Another Bulgari item in a 1960s design drawing from Maison Duhem, Paris, shows a similar bracelet with panthers' instead of lions' heads.

BELOW Two Bulgari designs for panther brooches in gold with enamel spots; one with onyx and turquoise, the other with onyx and coral.

RIGHT A page of Duhem's drawings for Bulgari shows three small animals impersonating humans.

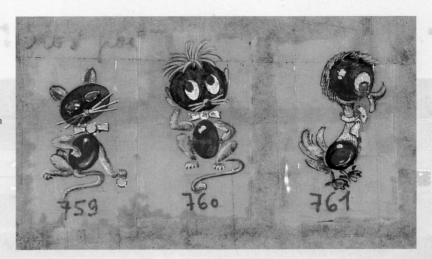

A variety of inventive animal sketches for jewels
from the Verdura Archives during the 1950s and '60s,
including not only the conventional creatures, such
as a cat, dogs and birds, but also a squirrel, a snail,
a porcupine and a giraffe.

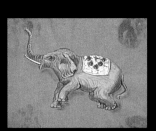

CL880

C 1165-II

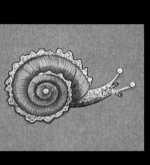

OPPOSITE Four catalogue covers from 1963 to 1966 for the Van Cleef & Arpels "La Boutique" line, which specialized in less expensive jewelry using primarily gold and semi-precious stones.

OPPOSITE AND ABOVE These fish clips by Van Cleef & Arpels, 1959, have bodies of cabochon sapphires with cabochon emerald eyes; the heads, fins and tails are pavé diamonds set in platinum. *Private collection. Photos Van Cleef & Arpels, Paris*

RIGHT A flying fish, also by Van Cleef & Arpels, 1957, has a body formed by a gray mabé pearl, mounted with gold fins and accented with diamonds, sapphires and a cabochon ruby eye. *Private collection. Photos Van Cleef & Arpels, Paris*

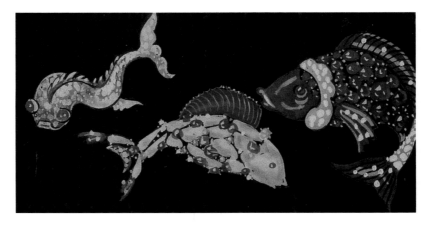

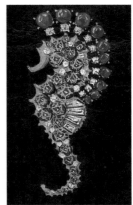

ABOVE Four samples of 1950s designs from the Seaman Schepps Archives, including fish brooches, a seahorse brooch and a snail.

BELOW Two diamond and emerald scorpion pins set in platinum, c. 1950, that belonged to Ingrid Bergman. *Photo Sotheby's, New York*

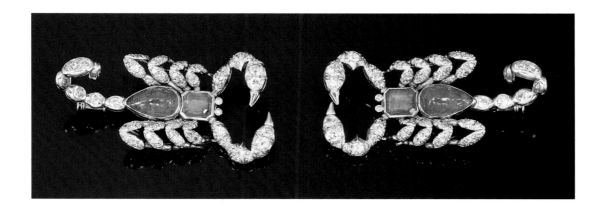

ABOVE A brooch by Boivin in the shape of intertwined dolphins, 1957, in yellow gold, emeralds and diamonds; and two 1950s sketches from the Archives for similar subjects suspending a round diamond drop. *Photo René Boivin*

RIGHT A 1985 design from the René Boivin Archives for a small tropical fish to be decorated with marquise emeralds and rubies.

BELOW RIGHT This dolphin brooch by Verdura from the 1960s was made of pavé-set diamonds in platinum with a head and tail of polished gold. *Photo Verdura, New York*

LEFT Jean Schlumberger's "Coral Star" brooch of 1956 was one of many signature starfish designs, the five points of the object recurring in both realistic starfish and abstract sea flowers. This example features coral cones mounted around a central platinum and diamond ribbon star. *Photo © Tiffany & Co.*

BELOW LEFT Schlumberger also designed these goldfish cufflinks with tiny emerald eyes during the 1960s for Tiffany & Co. *Private collection. Photo © GIA and Tino Hammid*

BELOW A fish brooch in 18K gold and watermelon tourmaline with cabochon aquamarine bubbles by Cartier, Paris, probably 1960s. *Photo courtesy Primavera Gallery, New York*

OPPOSITE This dolphin clip by Jean Schlumberger, 1964, was given to Elizabeth Taylor by Richard Burton and nicknamed "Iguana" since he had just completed filming *The Night of the Iguana*. The dolphin's mouth is outlined in calibré-cut emeralds, and the eyes are cabochon sapphires. *Collection Elizabeth Taylor. Photo © Tiffany & Co.*

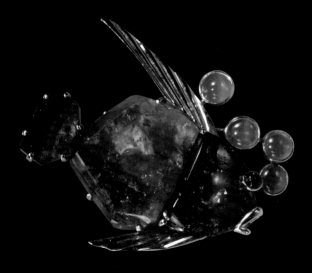

This articulated pearl, ruby, diamond and emerald starfish brooch, designed during the 1960s, has been attributed to Salvador Dalí. The undulating articulated arms can drape over a shoulder or around the hand with an attachment. Two butterfly enhancements accompany the jewel. *Photo Christie's, New York*

This jellyfish dress clip designed by Jean Schlumberger,
1965, and known as the "Medusa" was part of Mrs Paul
Mellon's collection. Cabochon moonstones are set among
prong-set diamonds in platinum to form the body, while
the tentacles are in rectangular-cut sapphires and flexible
gold cylinders. *Photo © Tiffany & Co.*

ABOVE This Cartier lizard brooch in diamonds and 18K gold is supposed to have been designed by Jeanne Toussaint for the French actress Jacqueline Delubac in 1958. The head, set with baguetate-cut diamonds on textured gold skin with an articulated tail, is moveable and tops the brilliant-cut yellowish-brown 11-stone spine. *Photo Christie's, Geneva*

LEFT A 1950s design from the Mauboussin Archives for a crocodile brooch in scored gold with calibré-cut sapphires, diamond and ruby accents.

OPPOSITE An imposing necklace commissioned from Cartier in 1968 by the Mexican actress Maria Felix. Set with diamonds in platinum and white gold, this piece has an ingenious circular diamond peg clasp, which holds it together at its crossover point. The reverse is decorated with alternating green, red and black enamel scales, and two emerald eyes peer out from the sides of the head. *Collection Art of Cartier. Photo Nick Welch © Cartier*

ABOVE LEFT A design from the Verdura Archives for a dragon brooch in gold with cabochon sapphire scales The feet and head are formed with platinum-set pavé diamonds and the tongue is made of coral.

ABOVE RIGHT A 1950 design from the René Boivin Archives for a pendant in yellow gold depicting a chimera with a sapphire-set body and marquise-shaped emerald-set wings.

LEFT A design from the Verdura Archives of the late 1950s for a brooch showing Cupid riding on the back of a domesticated turtle. The turtle has a gold and blue enamel shell and is adorned with a ruby collar on its platinum-set pavé diamond neck.

This bracelet of carved coral balls by Cartier, Paris, 1954, closes with an elaborate clasp in the form of a platinum and diamond chimera. *Collection Art of Cartier. Photo Nick Welch © Cartier*

ABOVE A brooch of a unicorn in the "Hawaii" style by Van Cleef & Arpels, New York, 1950. In polished gold, decorated with faceted rubies and a collar of faceted sapphires, the unicorn is perched on a bed of flowers. *Private collection. Photo Van Cleef & Arpels Paris*

BELOW Two 1950s designs for unicorn pins from the Verdura Archives.

ABOVE "Seabird" is the name of this clip in gold, platinum and pavé diamonds made by Jean Schlumberger in 1968. The fictional animal has a beak in black lacquer, a collar in blue enamel and a ruby eye. *Collection Margaret L. Burden. Photo © Tiffany and Co.*

RIGHT A unicorn clip by Jean Schlumberger from 1956, in pavé yellow beryls in gold, with a flowing mane of calibré-cut amethysts and brilliant-cut diamonds. The horn is a twisted gold rod. *Photo © Tiffany & Co.*

Chapter 6

1970s to the Present
Breaking New Ground – New Materials for a New Age

The economic uncertainty precipitated by the oil crisis in the 1970s brought about an uneasiness that was felt in all sectors of the economy. Because of this, the jewelry industry seemed temporarily to lose its sense of direction. In the absence of a cohesive trend guiding the major houses, a broad dichotomy of styles emerged. On the one hand, some favored minimalist designs such as "Diamonds-by-the-Yard", espoused by Tiffany's Elsa Peretti, i.e., diamonds set into gold mountings at intervals on a gold-link chain. Jewelry designed along these lines went with the dance-crazy disco scene of strobe lights and revolving mirrored balls that reflected the glittering stones. On the other hand, for those less "hip" but still wishing to be fashionable, large gemstones were mounted into either flexible wire settings or textured gold mountings. By the 1980s, disco was gone and the oil crisis had been resolved – resulting in a return to a stable economy. As elegant entertaining once again became the purview of society, with ladies dressing in the latest fashion and sporting lavish jewels, established jewelry concerns refocused their attention on beautiful pieces. Then, by the mid-1980s, a group of independent designers emerged that presaged a modern style for the new millennium. Throughout these dynamic times, one source of design inspiration, the animal motif, maintained a strong presence among the major houses as well as the new avant-garde designers.

Animal-style jewelry of the last three decades of the twentieth century took many different forms and was fabricated in traditional as well as non-traditional materials. The usual cast of characters in the animal kingdom received attention, but this period is also noted for some unusual – some might consider ugly – creatures that excited the imagination of talented designers. It was a time of experimentation, when jewelers explored new territories, when the traditional conception of beauty was still heeded but was now rendered in a freer, more relaxed way. What emerged was a fresh expression of the animal figures that jewelers had been replicating, analyzing, stylizing and beautifying for the past two hundred years – indeed, since Antiquity.

The butterfly that had been fluttering here and there finally landed. It was just as well that it did as its once delicate wings were now laden with heavy gem material. In a Van Cleef & Arpels brooch, the wings of the butterfly are formed with invisibly set sapphires, edged with diamonds. The same house accents their textured gold butterfly pins with a variety of gem material, such as lapis lazuli, malachite, onyx, chalcedony and tiger's eye. Beginning in 1983, Mauboussin developed a style of jewelry incorporating mother-of-pearl into the wings of birds and butterflies. Set into gold amid diamonds, this gem material "reflects moonlight in a sweet, clear fashion," or so ventured Marguerite de Cerval in her book *Mauboussin*.

In contrast to butterflies made with hard stones, Gianmaria Buccellati designed a more traditional, delicate insect with filigree wings set with pearls and diamonds, the body composed of a gray and a white pearl. In the 1990s, Ella Gafter at Ella Gems designed spiders with her signature stone, the South Sea pearl, for the body, and legs set with diamonds. Other creatures include a cricket from the house of Buccellati, with a textured gold body set with diamonds, and a dung beetle by John Paul Miller, a studio jeweler, who fashioned the insect out of gold decorated with enamel and granulation.

Perhaps the most innovative of all jewelry at the end of the twentieth century were those pieces created by Emmanuel and Sophie Guillaume for ESG Jewels in Geneva, that use not gold or platinum but a titanium alloy, a material originally developed for the aerospace industry. Although difficult to work with, titanium has a mechanical strength that makes possible thinner and lighter settings that are suitable for wearing on contemporary lightweight fabrics and also enable special effects. The Guillaumes made a dragonfly with matched Burmese rubies on the wings.

Bird jewelry was well represented in this most recent period. Jean Schlumberger placed a diamond-set bird on the top of a gemstone, at one time even the famous 128.54-carat Tiffany Diamond, and called it "Bird on a Rock". Superb examples by Van Cleef & Arpels include a stork carrying a 95-carat briolette diamond, once owned by the opera singer Ganna Walska, and a swan whose feathers are formed out of moonstones, an unusual gemstone for this venerable house where precious stones are the norm. Buccellati created that mythological bird, the phoenix. Its body is a 136.10-carat pearl (more precisely, a concretion of 17 pearl nuclei). A light-gray pearl drop pendant represents the ashes from which the bird rises again. The overall design recalls jewels from the Renaissance.

In 1979, pink diamonds were discovered in the Argyle pipe in the Western region of Australia, yielding a small but reliable supply of pink stones of less than half a carat. Several designers took advantage of these new colored diamonds to create animal-inspired jewels. In a brooch with a small and a large flamingo by jeweler Carvin French, different diamond cuts provide stunning imitations of the texture of the birds' bodies. He used circular cuts for the smooth surface of the neck and legs and marquise cuts for the coarser texture of the wing feathers. The artist Daniel Brush whimsically designed a bangle bracelet with a rabbit's head carved from a piece of pink Bakelite, a non-traditional material for fine jewelry. At the same time, many houses continued making animals in a

OPPOSITE A swan clip by Van Cleef & Arpels, 1970, made of textured gold with moonstone feathers. The bird's head is pavé diamonds set in platinum with emerald eyes. The neck and tail are studded with diamonds. *Photo Van Cleef and Arpels, Paris*

ABOVE The body of the phoenix in this brooch by Buccellati, 1983, is formed by a baroque pearl, and the feathers are made of yellow diamonds set in gold and colorless diamonds set in white gold. A natural pearl drop is suspended from the body. *Photo Buccellati*

BELOW Two of Ella Gafter's insect pins, 1998, made of South Sea pearls with diamonds. *Photo courtesy Ella Gems*

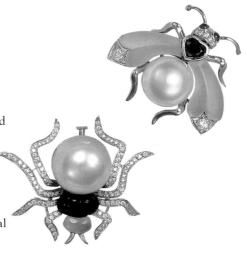

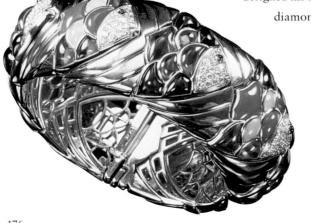

vein similar to previous designs, and what was big in terms of size in the '60s remained so for the rest of the century. Boivin continued their series of mammals, with amusing dogs (sometimes sitting in the doorway of a dog house), lions and elephants; Cartier reinvigorated the panther; and David Webb kept on making his animal jewelry with owls, tigers and dragons either enameled or diamond-set. Perhaps the most intriguing piece of animal jewelry designed by Van Cleef & Arpels during the latter decades was a crest with two rampant lions, each holding a scimitar, commissioned by the government of Iran as a gift for the Shah to commemorate the 2,500th anniversary of the founding of the Persian Empire.

Creatures from the sea seem to inspire some of the most imaginative jewelry designs. In the last three decades, some strange but enchanting creatures were put into jewelry form for the first time, some of them using unusual gem materials. Boivin tops the list. Imagine wearing a pavé-set pink tourmaline crayfish curled around a pear-shaped green tourmaline, or a yellow and white diamond octopus with cabochon emeralds on the tentacles. Marilyn Cooperman, who previously had to her credit aquatic figures with bodies of oxidized silver or gold set with pearls, created more than just another jewel when she designed "Fish Lunching on a Pearl". This undulating creature is pavé-set with various color sapphires on the body and carved emeralds for the fins and tail, while a pearl is suspended from its mouth, capped by several seaweed-like emeralds masking the about-to-be eaten juicy delight.

In 1991, Bulgari launched a series of *Naturalia* jewels to celebrate nature. Their characteristic style, distinguished by bold, striking color combinations, is evident in pieces from this series in which precious gemstones are juxtaposed with colored gemstones in stylized shapes derived from the animal world. Stylized fish swim in schools on earrings, or swim in single file around bracelets. Colorful stones form large scales in a mosaic-like effect.

The year 2000 was an exciting one for jewelry based on marine life, as talented jewelers on both sides of the Atlantic contributed outstanding designs. In Paris, the house of Mauboussin created a fish with an agate, accented with diamonds, and a squiggly jellyfish with opals, diamonds and enamel. In New York, Christopher Walling designed his first piece of jewelry from the animal kingdom, a fish with white and brown diamonds and grayish pink abalone pearls, the latter a trademark of his work.

Andreas von Zadora-Gerlof, who is known for exquisitely detailed sculptures of

ABOVE This bunny bangle by Daniel Brush, New York, 1988, is created out of pink Bakelite carved on the sides with images of a rabbit and a squirrel. The head and ears of the bunny resting on it are made of pink diamonds set with gold prongs. *Private collection*

BELOW LEFT In the early 1990s Bulgari created a group of *Naturalia* jewels based on animal designs. On this bangle bracelet fish are swimming end to end, their scales represented by alternating buff-cut coral, chalcedony, amethysts, citrines and tourmalines. *Photo Bulgari*

BELOW RIGHT These earrings by Bulgari, 1991, are called "*Mama Pesce*" ("Mother Fish") because the design shows a large fish followed by three small ones. *Photo Bulgari*

animals in gem material, has taken jewelry to a new level. Instead of creating a single piece of jewelry as an entity in itself, he developed the concept of incorporating pieces within sculptural groups. In an aquarium which hangs on the wall like a painting, he created a composition of undersea plant life and creatures carved from gem material or crafted in gold and enamel. This remarkable group functions on two levels. For pure visual enjoyment, the entire composition can be admired as a beautiful sculpture or painting; for personal adornment parts of it can be worn as jewelry.

The reptilian world has always held a fascination for designers and Zadora-Gerlof is no exception. He carved the hard shell of a large sea turtle brooch from a citrine, the color complemented by brown diamonds on the fins and the head. Towards the end of the twentieth century, snakes from the previous century were transformed into a modern idiom. Bulgari wrapped them around wrists as enameled and diamond-set bracelet watches. ESG Jewels created an articulated snake necklace with 3,750 Montana sapphires, each stone chosen for its unique color tones. Joel Arthur Rosenthal, better known as JAR, dramatically winds a snake around a woman's neck. With its head slightly cocked and its tail slightly flipped upwards, it comes as close to replicating the actual serpent as is possible in jewelry.

As if it wasn't sufficiently adventurous to have one snake wrapped about one's neck, Cartier took this theme one step further, substituting the snake with two alligators. Commissioned in 1975 by Maria Felix, the alligator necklace was designed by Gabriel Raton, who had earlier created an unusual snake necklace for the same client. On this highly unusual necklace, one alligator is set with 1,023 fancy colored yellow diamonds while the other is set with 1,066 emeralds – a spectacular piece of jewelry in both its design and the number of gemstones lavished on it. Cartier also resurrected the lizard from the nineteenth century; but instead of depicting it on a brooch crawling about the ground, it now walks around the wrist, forming a bracelet.

Figurative jewelry in animal shapes has become a mainstay of the jeweler's art. It has evolved from stiff representations of wild life to imaginative depictions of just about every creature from the animal kingdom. As the twenty-first century proceeds, designers will continue to set aside past constraints and explore new domains; perhaps creatures from an as yet unexplored planet will be their grist as they look for new models in their never ending quest for beauty. Animals capture our fancy, cause us to smile, and help us to broaden our appreciation and enjoyment of what nature has to offer. May we be confident that talented and creative jewelers will continue to enhance that enjoyment with the products of their inspired craft.

This flexible snake watch made in the 1970s by Bulgari uses gold, black enamel and diamonds. The pavé diamond head with pear-shaped ruby eyes lifts to reveal the dial. *Photo Bulgari*

This "Bird on a Rock" clip brooch was made in 1995 from a 1975 model by Jean Schlumberger. The bird, made in platinum-set pavé diamonds and gold-set pavé yellow diamonds, is perched on the 128.54-carat Tiffany yellow diamond. *Photo © Tiffany & Co.*

ABOVE This demantoid butterfly in titanium alloy was completed by ESG Jewels of Geneva in 1999. It had taken seven years to collect the 349 gem demantoids weighing 40.44 carats. The piece also contains 120 tsavorites for 2.56 carats and 522 diamonds for 2.93 carats. Being made of titanium, the butterfly has only 4.9 grams of metal and is very lightweight. *Private collection. Photo by Harold and Erica Van Pelt*

OPPOSITE A page from the 1976 "La Boutique" catalogue issued by Van Cleef & Arpels that features butterfly pins in textured gold, diamonds and various hardstones, such as lapis lazuli, coral, malachite, tiger's eye, onyx and chalcedony. *Van Cleef & Arpels Archives*

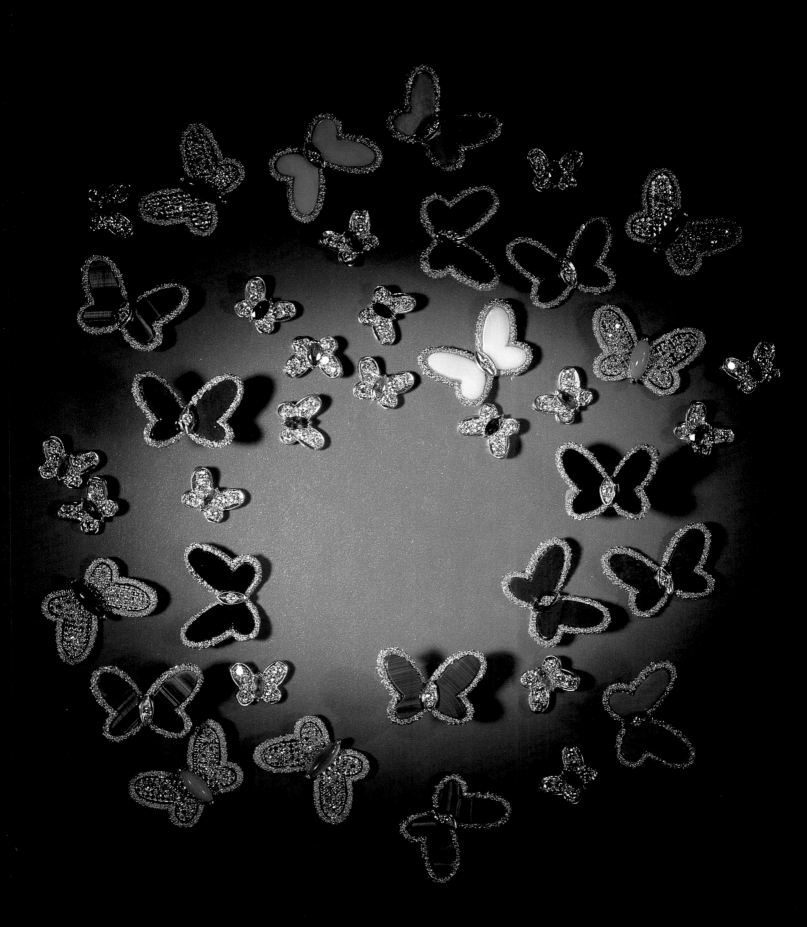

Mauboussin has produced many jewels in the form of butterflies. Above is a 1992 brooch of in gold, mother-of-pearl, diamonds and cabochon rubies, and below are three varied butterfly designs from the Mauboussin Archives.

The body of this butterfly clip by Van
Cleef & Arpels, 1973, is made of marquise
diamonds set in platinum with invisibly set
sapphires. *Photo Van Cleef & Arpels, Paris*

It was in 1999 that Buccellati produced this
butterfly brooch with a body made of a white
freshwater pearl and a gray baroque pearl. The
wings are white and yellow gold filigree studded
with diamonds and pearls. *Photo Buccellati*

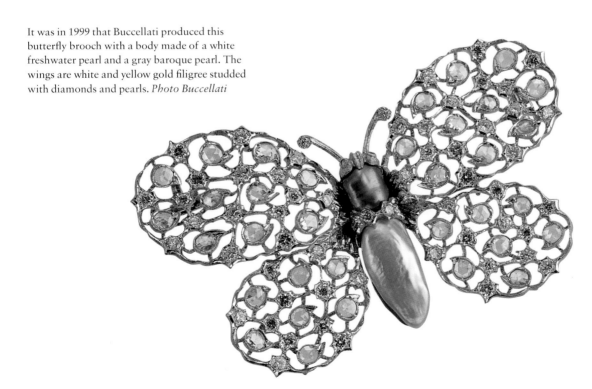

This elaborate dragonfly brooch, produced by ESG Jewels of Geneva in 2000, consists of rubies and diamonds set in titanium alloy. Weighing less than 22 grams, the body is composed of a line of gem quality rubies (over 37 carats in all), as are the wings. The pavé diamond setting extends around to the back side of the body. *Photo Sotheby's, New York*

OPPOSITE A necklace with a beetle pendant by
the American designer John Paul Miller, 1989.
Drawing on the ancient Etruscan art of granulation,
a process whereby tiny gold balls are fused onto a gold
background through a process of molecular exchange,
he combines this technique with cloisonné enamel for
a unique result. *Photo courtesy of the designer*

ABOVE This brooch made by ESG Jewels, Geneva, 2000,
depicts a large flower in fancy intense yellow diamonds
pavé-set in 18K gold, with a snail crawling up the pavé
emerald stem. The snail's body is set with grayish
diamonds in white gold. The jewel is over 4 inches
in length. *Photo © GIA and Tino Hammid.*

RIGHT The realistic cricket brooch by Buccellati, 1975, is
made of textured gold and diamonds. *Photo Buccellati*

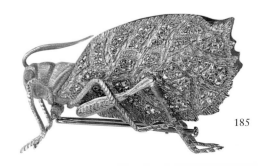

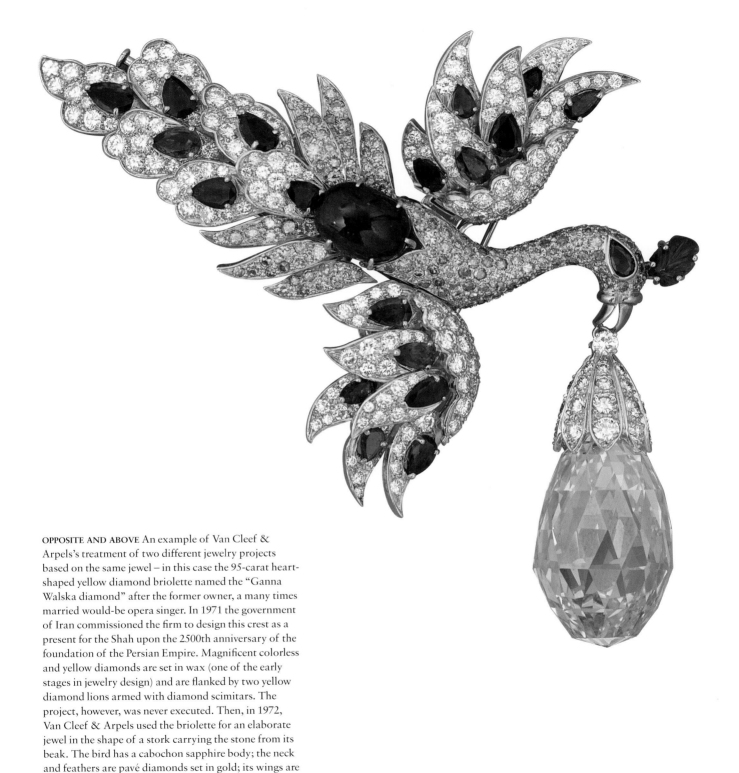

OPPOSITE AND ABOVE An example of Van Cleef & Arpels's treatment of two different jewelry projects based on the same jewel – in this case the 95-carat heart-shaped yellow diamond briolette named the "Ganna Walska diamond" after the former owner, a many times married would-be opera singer. In 1971 the government of Iran commissioned the firm to design this crest as a present for the Shah upon the 2500th anniversary of the foundation of the Persian Empire. Magnificent colorless and yellow diamonds are set in wax (one of the early stages in jewelry design) and are flanked by two yellow diamond lions armed with diamond scimitars. The project, however, was never executed. Then, in 1972, Van Cleef & Arpels used the briolette for an elaborate jewel in the shape of a stork carrying the stone from its beak. The bird has a cabochon sapphire body; the neck and feathers are pavé diamonds set in gold; its wings are made of diamonds and pear-shaped emeralds; its crest is a carved emerald and another pear-shaped emerald forms the eye. *Photos Van Cleef & Arpels, Paris*

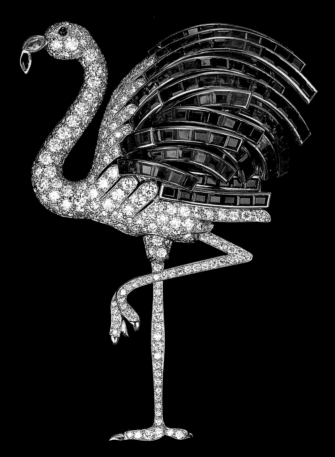

LEFT Flamingo brooch by Cartier, Paris, 1987, made from the original 1939 design and under the patronage of Fanny Jacqueau, daughter of Cartier's famous designer Charles Jacqueau. A replica of the Duchess of Windsor's well-known bird, this piece proves that fine workmanship still existed in the late 20th century. The flamingo proudly stands on its hinged platinum and diamond leg, flaunting the colorful wings of calibré-cut emeralds, rubies and sapphires. *Private collection. Photo © GIA and Tino Hammid*

OPPOSITE Another example of the flamingo theme is the brooch opposite, designed by Carvin French, New York, 1996. The bodies of each of the two birds are set with circular, marquise and pear-shaped pink diamonds, while faceted black diamonds form their beaks. They stand in a demantoid garnet marsh. *Photo Christie's, New York*

Two 1972 designs from the René Boivin Archives for eagle brooches in gold, oxidized silver, diamonds, sapphires, emeralds and rubies.

The Boivin Archives contain many designs for elephant pendants and clips from 1940 through to 1980. On the left is a pendant in gold and yellow diamonds based on a design from the Archives. The other drawings call for gold and jeweled regalia in the Indian style, but the black elephant was designed in ebony.

Four 1970s designs of dachshunds in gold and yellow diamonds with onyx eyes, from the René Boivin Archives.

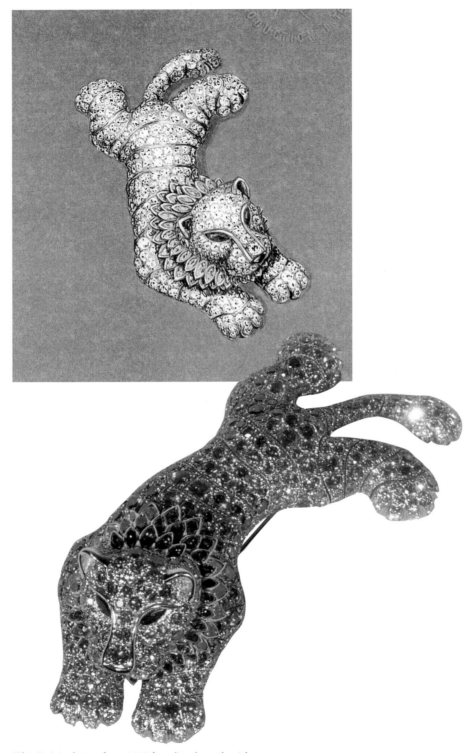

This Boivin design from 1960 for a lion brooch with
an articulated body and legs set with brilliant-cut
diamonds was made in 1993 as a jewel in yellow
diamonds. The mane is designed with marquise-cut
yellow diamonds and the eyes are marquise emeralds.
Photo René Boivin

A novel approach by Boivin to panther jewelry presents
a leopard skin laid out like a carpet. This example, made
from a 1957 design and produced in 1993, is a clip made of
gold, yellow diamonds and onyx. It is entirely flexible and
can be worn draped over the shoulder. *Photos René Boivin*

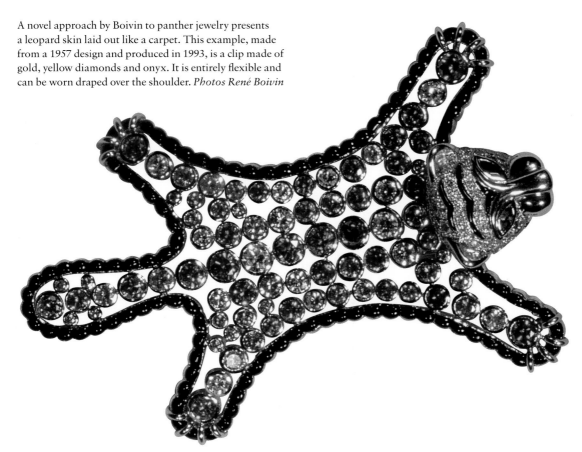

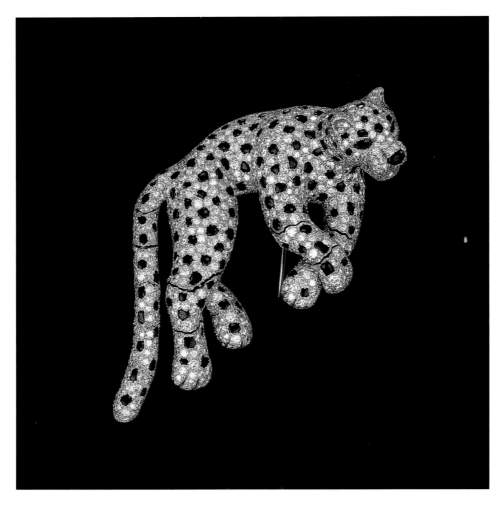

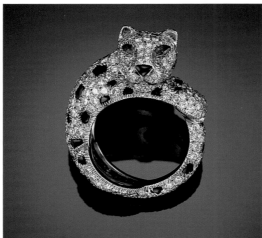

Two panther jewels by Cartier, Paris, 1981, in platinum and pavé diamonds with black onyx spots and emerald eyes. The brooch features articulated legs and tail with a rotating head. *Private collection. Photos © GIA and Tino Hammid*

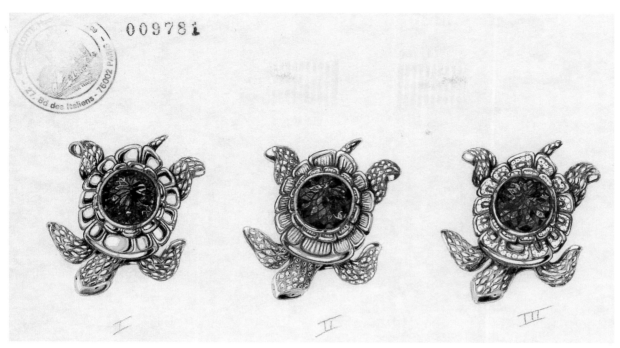

ABOVE AND RIGHT The turtle pin at right, by Boivin, 1992, is made in gold and diamonds with a shell of faceted citrine. It is accompanied by three designs with shells in faceted amethysts. *Photo René Boivin*

BELOW Designs made by Donald Claflin in the early 1970s for two animal brooches constructed around large rectangular amethysts. The elephant is decorated in full jeweled Indian regalia, and the turtle holds a flower in its mouth. *Tiffany & Co. Archives*

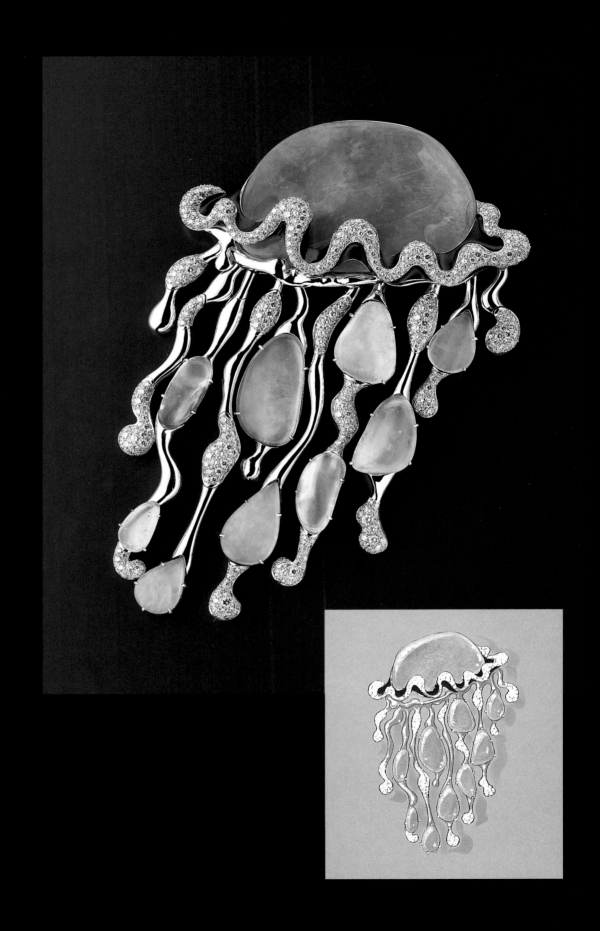

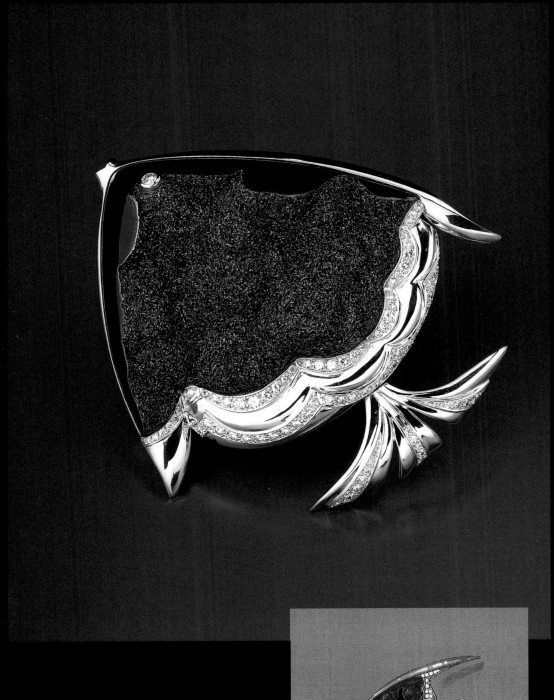

OPPOSITE One of Mauboussin's creations in 2000 was a jellyfish brooch in white gold, diamonds, black enamel and opals. It is accompanied here by a gouache design of the clip. *Photo Mauboussin*

ABOVE In experimenting with the use of new materials in 2000, Mauboussin designed and produced this fish clip centering a glittered agate set in white gold with diamonds. *Photo Mauboussin*

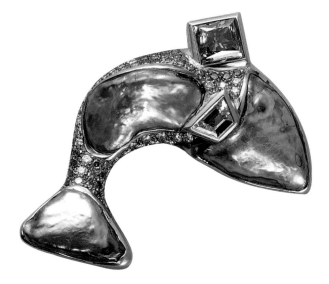

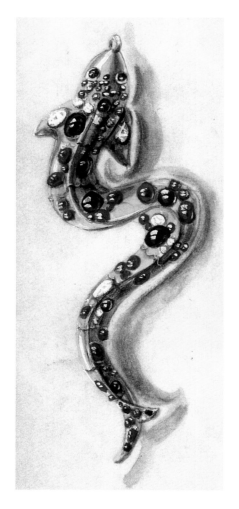

LEFT A 1975 design from the René Boivin Archives for a pendant in the shape of an eel in cabochon sapphires and diamonds with cabochon ruby eyes set in gold.

ABOVE This brooch in the form of an abstract fish was made in 2000 by Christopher Walling. It is constructed around three baroque pearls set in 18K gold; the eye is suggested by a round imperfection on the triangular-shaped baroque pearl used for the head. The body is made of brownish pavé-set diamonds surrounding a large curved baroque pearl, while the gill is a trapezoid-shaped brown diamond and the fin is a square radiant-cut brown diamond. *Photo by Matthew Klein*

BELOW This design for a brooch depicting a crayfish in yellow gold with pavé pink tourmalines and diamonds is from the René Boivin Archives, 1985.

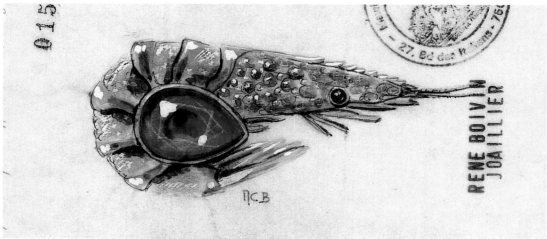

RIGHT The curving body of this fish brooch by Marilyn Cooperman, New York, 1994, is composed of brilliant-cut sapphires set in yellow and gray gold, while the fins and tail are made of carved emeralds. The fish suspends from its mouth a pearl drop set with carved emeralds.
Photo courtesy Marilyn Cooperman, New York

BELOW A drawing from the René Boivin Archives, 1993, for a brooch in the shape of a salmon in yellow gold, pink tourmalines and diamonds.

René Boivin designed this elaborate octopus brooch
of yellow gold set with yellow and colorless diamonds
in 1993. The tentacles are represented by bezel-set
cabochon emeralds and the legs are articulated.
Photo René Boivin

ABOVE A sea turtle brooch by Andreas von Zadora-Gerlof, 2000, in gold with brown diamonds set on the fins and head. The shell is a carved citrine accented with bezel-set diamond studs, and the eyes are cabochon sapphires. The fins are attached to the body with titanium springs, thus allowing them to move *en tremblant. Photo by David Behl*

RIGHT This aquarium was designed by Zadora in 1999 as an undersea painting displaying ten pieces of jewelry, which the client can enjoy *in situ* or take out and wear as brooches or earrings. The frame is carved in lapis lazuli, and the various sea creatures are made in 18K gold, translucent enamel, opalescent enamel, carved citrines, carved green beryl and carved multicolored fluorite. *Photo by David Behl*

A group of 18K gold and polychrome enamel cufflinks
made in the 1990s by Nick Loz for SST, Los Angeles.
Featuring various animal motifs, including fish, insects,
penguins, dogs and African big game beasts, each side
of the cufflink represents a different animal.
Photo © GIA and Tino Hammid

This dragon bangle by David Webb, c. 1980, is made
of gold, black enamel, diamonds and emeralds. The
dragon grips a diamond ring connected to its tail.
Photo Christie's, New York

A chimera bangle bracelet by Cartier, Paris, 1970,
in which the mythological beast is carved in coral
and set with platinum and diamond accents.
Private collection. Photo © GIA and Tino Hammid

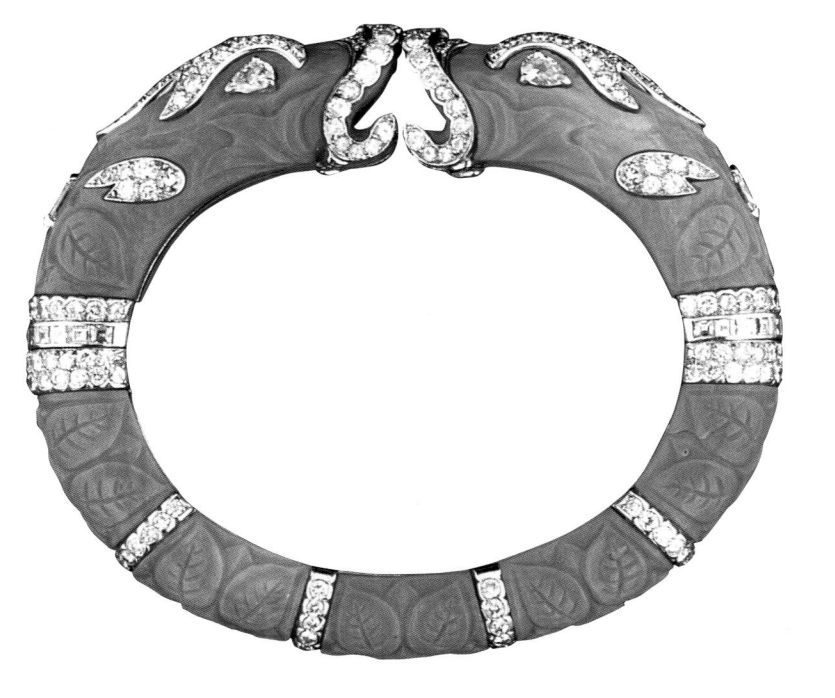

RIGHT This bangle bracelet by Cartier, Paris, 1972, consists of a lizard that encircles the wrist with its head, tail and body. The scales are artfully created in yellow diamonds, sapphires and emeralds set in yellow gold. The feet are pavé diamonds and yellow diamonds; the eyes are cabochon rubies. *Collection Art of Cartier. Photo Nick Welch © Cartier*

BELOW A 1980s choker in the form of a serpent by JAR, Paris, that was the property of the French actress Jacqueline Delubac. With a circular-cut sapphire centered on the head and surrounded by pavé-set diamonds set in silver-topped gold, the creature displays its snakeskin pattern with centrally set amethysts in pavé-set sapphires. *Photo Christie's, Geneva*

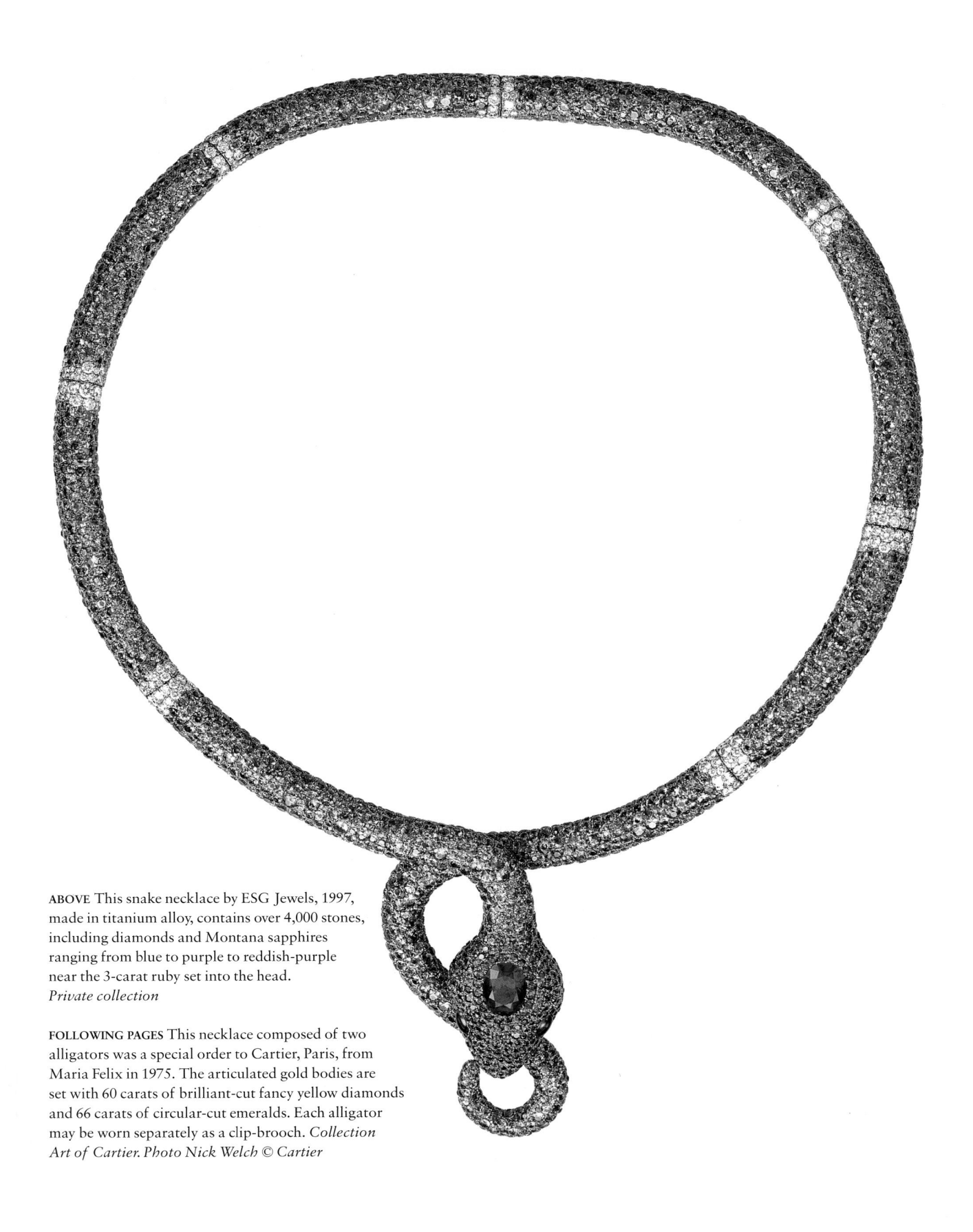

ABOVE This snake necklace by ESG Jewels, 1997, made in titanium alloy, contains over 4,000 stones, including diamonds and Montana sapphires ranging from blue to purple to reddish-purple near the 3-carat ruby set into the head. *Private collection*

FOLLOWING PAGES This necklace composed of two alligators was a special order to Cartier, Paris, from Maria Felix in 1975. The articulated gold bodies are set with 60 carats of brilliant-cut fancy yellow diamonds and 66 carats of circular-cut emeralds. Each alligator may be worn separately as a clip-brooch. *Collection Art of Cartier. Photo Nick Welch © Cartier*

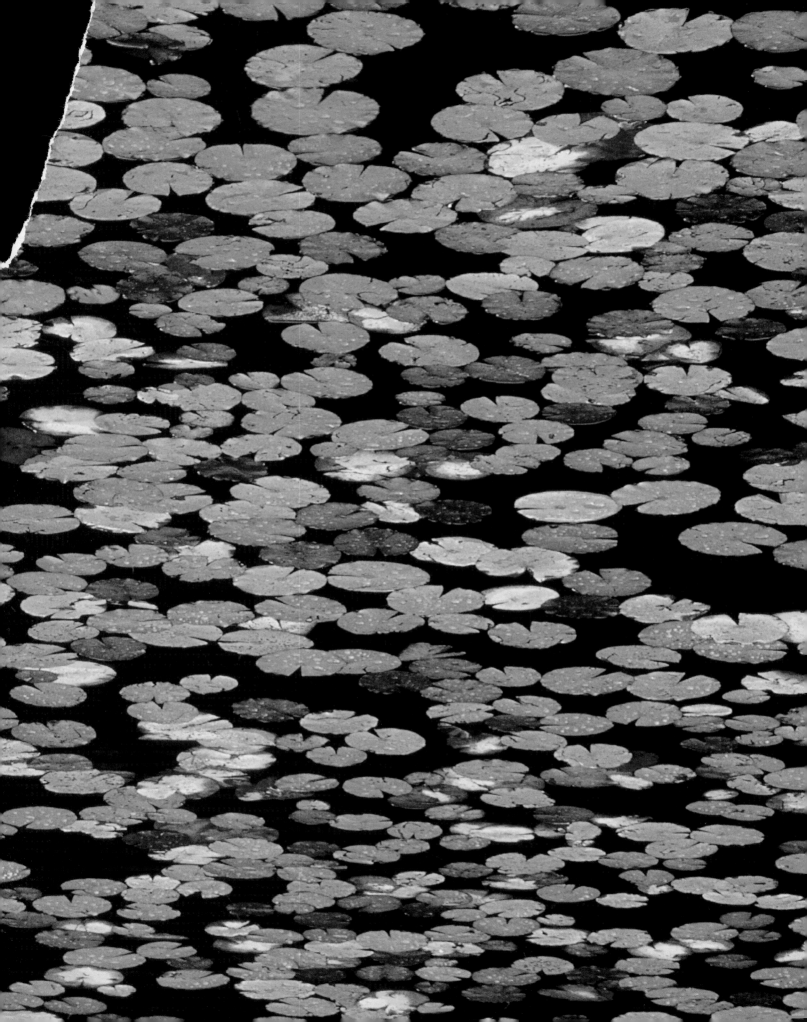

Bibliography

Aldred, Cyril, *Jewels of the Pharaohs. Egyptian Jewelry of the Dynastic Period*, New York and Washington 1991.

Andrews, Carol, *Amulets of Ancient Egypt*, Austin 1994.

— *Ancient Egyptian Jewelry*, New York 1991.

Arwas, Victor, *Art Deco*, New York 1980.

Becker, Vivienne, *Antique and Twentieth-Century Jewellery. A Guide for Collectors* (2nd edition), Colchester, Essex, 1987.

— *Art Nouveau Jewelry*, New York, 1985.

— *The Jewellery of Rene Lalique* (a Goldsmiths' Company Exhibition, London, May 28–July 24, 1987).

Bennett, David and Daniela Mascetti, *Understanding Jewellery*, Woodbridge, Suffolk, 1994.

Bizot, Chantal and Evelyne Possémé, Marie-Noël de Gary, Olivier Brandily, *Un Diamant dans la Ville. Jean Schlumberger 1907–1987 Bijoux-Objets* (exhibition at the Musée des Arts Décoratifs, Paris, October 19, 1995–February 25, 1996).

Brunhammer, Yvonne, ed., *The Jewels of Lalique* (catalogue of an exhibition at The Cooper-Hewitt National Design Museum, Smithsonian Institution, New York, February 3–April 12, 1998; International Gallery, Smithsonian Institution, Washington, D.C., May 15–August 16, 1998; and Dallas Museum of Art, September 13, 1998–January 10, 1999).

Brunhammer, Yvonne, *et al.*, *Rene Lalique. Jewelry, Glass* (catalogue of an exhibition at the Musée des Arts Décoratifs, Paris, October 22, 1991–March 8, 1992).

Buccellati, Maria Cristina, ed., *Buccellati. Art in Gold, Silver and Gems*, Milan 2000.

Burollet, Thérèse, Gilles Chazal and Nathalie Morigeon, *The Art of Cartier* (exhibition at the Musée du Petit Palais, Paris, October 20, 1989–January 28, 1990).

Cailles, Françoise (tr. Tanya Leslie), *René Boivin, Jeweller*, London 1994.

Cartlidge, Barbara, *Twentieth-Century Jewelry*, New York 1985.

De Cerval, Marguerite, *Mauboussin*, Paris 1992.

Clair, Jean, *et al.*, *Lost Paradise: Symbolist Europe*, (exhibition at the Montreal Museum of Fine Arts, June 8–October 15, 1995).

Cologni, Franco and Eric Nussbaum, *Platinum by Cartier. Triumphs of the Jewelers' Art*, New York 1996.

Corgnati, Martina, *Mario Buccellati, Prince of Goldsmiths*, New York 1999.

Dietz, Ulysses Grant, Jenna Weissman Joselit, Kevin J. Smead, Janet Zapata, *The Glitter and the Gold: Fashioning America's Jewelry*, Newark 1997.

Duncan, Alastair, ed., *The Encyclopedia of Art Deco. An Illustrated Guide to a Decorative Style from 1920 to 1939*, New York 1988.

Eleuteri, Lodovica Rizzoli, ed., *Twentieth-Century Jewelry*, Milan and New York 1994.

Esmerian, Ralph, Paul Theroux, Donald Kuspit, David Bennett and Daniel Brush, *Daniel Brush: Gold Without Boundaries*, New York 1998.

Farkas, Ann and Boris Piotrovsky, *From the Lands of the Scythians. Ancient Treasures from the Museums of the U.S.S.R. 300 BC–100 BC*, New York and Los Angeles, 1975.

Ferreira, Maria Teresa Gomes, *Lalique Jóias*, Lisbon 1997.

Gabardi, Melissa, *Art Deco Jewellery 1920–1949*, Woodbridge, Suffolk, 1989.

— *Les Bijoux des Annees '50*, Milan 1987.

— *Gioielli Anni '40*, Milan 1982.

Gabriel, Jeanette Hanisee, with contributions by Anna Maria Massinelli, Judy Rudoe and Massimo Alfieri, *The Gilbert Collection Micromosaics*, London 2000.

Garside, Anne, ed., *Jewelry Ancient to Modern*, New York 1979.

Gary, Marie-Noël de, *Les Fouquet: Bijoutiers et Joailliers à Paris 1860–1960*, Paris 1983.

— *I gioielli degli anni '20–'40 Cartier e I grandi del Déco* (exhibition at Palazzo Fortuny, Venice, September 7–November 2, 1986).

Hackenbroch, Yvonne, *Renaissance Jewellery*, London, 1979.

Hapsburg, Geza von, *Fabergé*, Geneva 1987.

Harlow, George, ed., *The Nature of Diamonds*, Cambridge 1998.

Higgins, Reynold, *Greek and Roman Jewellery* (2nd edition), Berkeley and Los Angeles 1980.

Hinks, Peter, *Nineteenth-Century Jewellery*, London 1975.

— *Twentieth-Century British Jewellery 1900–1980*, London 1983.

Jutheau, Viviane, *Sterlé: Joaillier, Paris*, Paris 1990.

Kilbride-Jones, Howard, *Zoomorphic Penannular Brooches*, London 1980.

Koch, Michael, Evelyne Possémé, Judy Rudoe, Geoffrey Munn, Marie-Noël de Gary, Barbara Furrer, Cathérine Arminjon and Alexander Herzog von Württemberg, *The Belle Epoque of French Jewellery 1850–1910*, London 1991.

Levine, Gilbert and Laura L. Vookles, *The Jeweler's Eye. Nineteenth-Century Jewelry in the Collection of Nancy and Gilbert Levine*, (catalogue for exhibition at The Hudson River Museum, Yonkers, New York, October 5, 1986–January 4, 1987).

Lightbown, Ronald W., *Medieval European Jewellery*, London 1992.

Loring, John, *Tiffany Jewels*, New York 1999.

— *Tiffany's 20th Century. A Portrait of American Style*, New York 1997.

Lurker, Manfred, *The Gods and Symbols of Ancient Egypt. An Illustrated Dictionary*, London 1991.

Mascetti, Daniela and Amanda Triossi, *Bulgari*, Milan 1996.

Munn, Geoffrey, *Castellani and Giuliano. Revivalist Jewellers of the 19th Century*, New York 1984.

— *The Triumph of Love. Jewelry 1530–1930*, London and New York 1993.

Nadelhoffer, Hans, *Cartier, Jewelers Extraordinary*, New York and London 1984.

Néret, Gilles, *Boucheron. Four Generations of a World-Renowned Jeweler*, New York 1988.

Newberry, Percy E., *Scarabs. An Introduction to the Study of Egyptian Seals and Signet Rings*, London 1906.

Newman, Harold, *An Illustrated Dictionary of Jewelry*, London 1981.

Nissenson, Marilyn and Susan Jonas, *Jeweled Bugs and Butterflies*, New York 2000.

— *Snake Charm*, New York 1995.

Papi, Stefano and Alexandra Rhodes, *Famous Jewelry Collectors*, London and New York 1999.

Phillips, Clare, *Jewels and Jewellery*, London 2000.

Proddow, Penny and Marion Fasel, *Diamonds. A Century of Spectacular Jewels*, New York 1996.

Proddow, Penny and Debra Healy, *American Jewelry. Glamour and Tradition*, New York 1987.

Proddow, Penny and Marion Fasel, *Hollywood Jewels: Movies, Jewelry, Stars*, New York 1992.

Purcell, Katherine, *Falize: A Dynasty of Jewelers*, London and New York 1999.

— *Henri Vever's French Jewelry of the Nineteenth Century*, London and New York, 2001.

Raulet, Sylvie, *Art Deco Jewelry*, New York 1985.

— *Jewelry of the 1940s and 1950s*, New York 1988.

— *Van Cleef & Arpels*, New York 1987.

Rudoe, Judy, *Cartier 1900–1939*, New York 1997.

Vreeland, Diana, Jean d'Ormesson, Charlotte Gere and Vivienne Becker, and Franco Maria Ricci (ed.), *Jean Schlumberger*, Milan 1991.

Sataloff, Joseph, *Art Nouveau Jewelry*, Bryn Mawr, 1984.

Snowman, A. Kenneth, ed., *The Master Jewelers*, New York 1990.

Tait, Hugh, ed., *Jewelry 7000 Years. An International History and Illustrated Survey from the Collections of the British Museum*, New York 1986.

Traina, John, *Extraordinary Jewels*, New York 1994.

Williams, Dyfri and Jack Ogden, *Greek Gold Jewelry of the Classical World*, New York 1994.

Zapata, Janet, *The Art of Zadora, America's Fabergé*, New York 1999.

— *The Jewelry and Enamels of Louis Comfort Tiffany*, London and New York 1993.

Acknowledgments

This book would not have been possible without the assistance of many individuals who contributed so much in turning an idea into a reality. We are especially indebted to Michael Tennenbaum for making it all possible. We would like to thank Ricardo Zapata for his constant editorial assistance. We are grateful to Carol Doumani for her help in devising a strategy to find a publisher; Elise Misiorowski at the Gemological Institute of America and Tino Hammid for their collaboration on photographing many pieces of jewelry; Alice Carter and Sandra Kuenhert for their indispensable secretarial help; and Susan Jonas and Marilyn Nissenson for providing one of their books when it seemed impossible to find.

A book with so many photographs required the support of many friends and colleagues. Without their aid, it would have been impossible to locate the wide assortment of images required for the book. For this we would like to thank Benedicte Martin du Daffoy, Ralph Esmerian, Giuseppe Torroni, Dr Joseph and Ruth Sataloff, and the artist Daniel Brush.

We especially thank Robert I. Weingarten who allowed us to use his photographs of nature scenes as background for jewelry.

Museums are a repository for great works of art, including jewelry. We are grateful that many of these institutions collected superb examples of animal-inspired jewelry that we were able to use in this book. Museum staff members helpful in providing material as well as in suggesting other images for the book are Donald Peirce and Keith D. Knox, High Museum of Art, Atlanta; Takeo Horiuchi, Louis Tiffany Garden Museum, Matsue, Japan; Maria Fernanda Passos, Museu Calouste Gulbenkian, Lisbon; Ulysses G. Dietz and William Peniston, Newark Museum; Roger Berkowitz and Lee Mooney, Toledo Museum of Art; Frederick R. Brandt and Howell Perkins, Virginia Museum of Fine Arts, Richmond; and William Johnston and Cynthia Pratt, The Walters Art Museum, Baltimore.

Gallery owners in both the United States and Europe generously provided invaluable illustrative material. We are grateful to the following for their support: Ulf Breede, Breede, Berlin and Munich; Camilla Dietz Bergeron and Gus Davis, Camilla Dietz Bergeron, Ltd., New York; Sandra Cronan, Sandra Cronan, Ltd., London; Carlo Eleuteri, Carlo Eleuteri, Rome and Milan; Fred Leighton and Prema O'Grady, Fred Leighton, Ltd., New York and Las Vegas; David Firestone and Edwin Firestone, Firestone & Parson, Boston; Harriet Stein, HMS Ltd., Beverly Hills; Denis Gallion and Daniel Morris, Historical Design, New York; Joan Munves-Boeing, James Robinson, Inc., New York; Janet Mavec and Diane Lewis, J. Mavec & Co., New York; Barbara Macklowe and Benjamin Macklowe, Macklowe Gallery and Modernism, New York; Neil Lane, Neil Lane Jewelry, Los Angeles; Andrew Nelson, Malcolm Logan and David Johanson, Nelson Rarities, Inc., Portland, Maine; Audrey Friedman, Primavera Gallery, New York; Stefan Richter, Richters, Palm Beach; Filippo Villa, Villa Gioielliere, Milan; and Geoffrey C. Munn and Katherine Purcell, Wartski, London.

Many archivists, historians and designers from large and small jewelry houses were helpful not only with material from the past but also with images from the present. We would like to thank them for allowing us access to their files and for providing photographs: Michel Tonnelot, Boucheron, Paris; Howard M. Hyde, Buccellati, New York; Selman Arat, Bulgari, New York; Eric Nussbaum and Betty Jais, Cartier, Geneva and Paris; André Chervin, Carvin French, New York; Marilyn F. Cooperman, Marilyn F. Cooperman, Inc., New York; Pierre-Edouard Duhem and Jean-Claude Duhem, Maison Duhem, Paris; Ella and Talila Gafter, Ella Gems, New York; Emmanuel Guillaume and Sophie Guillaume, ESG Jewels, Geneva; Marguerite de Cerval, Mauboussin, Paris; Anne-Laurence Imbert, Mellerio, Paris; John Paul Miller; Sylvie Vilein and Christine Albasini, Poiray for René Boivin, Paris; Anna Marie Sandecki, Louisa Bann, Linda Buckley and Pierce B. MacGuire, Tiffany & Co., Parsippany, New Jersey and New York; François Arpels, François Canavey and Catherine Ficaja, Van Cleef & Arpels, Paris; Ward Landrigan, Verdura, New York; Roshi Ameri, Seaman Schepps, New York; Robert Gibson, Raymond Yard, New York; Christopher Walling, Christopher Walling Inc., New York; and Andreas von Zadora-Gerlof, Zadora, New York.

Animal-inspired jewelry frequently is sold at auctions. We would like to thank the following for furnishing important photographic material for this book: Simon Teakle, Christie's; Jane Padelford, Christie's Images; Danielle Turian, Alexandra Rhodes, Valerie Vlasaty, Sotheby's; and Dora Blary and Frederic Chambre, Calmels, Chambre, Cohen, Paris.

We would like to thank Constance Kaine and Sam Clark at Thames & Hudson for their artful arrangement of the photographs in the book. We thank Claire Stockfisch and Kate Slotover for their sharp-eyed proofreading. We are especially indebted to our editor at Thames & Hudson, Stanley Baron, who believed in this book, provided valuable editorial direction and patiently worked with us to resolve the inevitable problems that crept up along the way.

Suzanne Tennenbaum
Janet Zapata

Index

Photo Credits

Background Photographs

We are happy to include the following statement by Robert I. Weingarten, whose photographs appear as backgrounds on pp. 4–5 (*Morning Fog #2*, Pebble Beach, 2000), pp. 26–27 (*Lavender Field and Lone Tree*, Provence, 1999), pp. 28–29 (*Lichen at Cumbria*, Cumbria, 1996), pp. 60–61 (*Palouse Pattern #3*, Washington State, 2000), pp. 134–35 (*Expansive Tree*, near Malibu, 2000), p. 140 (*Spotlit Tree #2*, near Malibu, 2000), pp. 144–45 (*Driftwood*, Big Sur, 1999), and pp. 208–09 (*Waterlilies*, Hudson Valley, 2000).

Henri Cartier-Bresson has spoken of "the decisive moment" in creating a photo-journalistic image; a unique instant that is different from any other and captured for posterity in a fraction of a second.

When one thinks of landscape photography, it is perceived in much more languorous terms: slowly executed, contemplative, still. But this is usually not the case. Though the preparation can take hours, days or longer, with the light and mood constantly changing and evolving, there is indeed a "decisive moment" that captures the essence of a landscape.

I try to make my images reflect the timelessness of the landscape and at the same time the fleeting nature of a particular confluence of light and conditions that render a dramatic and signal moment; a sense of being there – the sights, the sounds, the smells, the feel of the air – on to a two-dimensional plane – a still image – with the hope that the ultimate viewer will experience what I felt.

It has been asked whether a photographic image is a window or a mirror. Does it show you simply what the photographer saw or does it also give you insight into the emotions of the image maker? I hope my images do both.